What dog owners are saying about Vera Reeves:

Vera is incredible! She really understands dogs and what makes them tick. She's great fun to work with.

— *Margot Holtzman with Lola; San Rafael, CA*

Vera's most important quality as a trainer (besides her vast knowledge) is her honesty and her caring about dog and owner.

— *Peggy Moore with Fenian; Ashland, OR*

I was at my wits end with a pile of dog-training books, advice from vets, and trainers, and a dog who just wouldn't train. Then Vera was recommended and suddenly I got it. Now my dog is well trained and we have a wonderful connection.

— *Susan Robinson with Schooner; Point Reyes, CA*

Vera Reeves is one of those exceptional trainers who understand how dogs think.

— *Catherine Rice with Coco; Novato, CA*

Vera makes the training fun for the dogs and their humans. Your dog may not even realize he is being trained!

— *Maggie Hall with Riley; Napa, CA*

I came to Vera as a last resort. My Australian Sheepdog mix, Casey, failed several classes because he was aggressive and uncontrollable. I had heard that Vera carried a reputation for turning out-of-control dogs around. Although I kept waiting for her to recommend that I just have Casey put down (as had been suggested to me), she didn't. Instead, she let me know that I needed to unlearn everything I was taught about dog training.

Vera worked a miracle! Casey is happy, well-adjusted, bonded to me and completely reliable off leash. In obedience, he is clearly running circles around his former classmates. He is a pleasure to have around now and I can't thank Vera enough for her dedication and skill in training dogs.

— *Pat Manley with Casey; Berkeley, CA*

My experience with Vera has been wonderful for both of my Rott-weilers and myself.

— *Barbie Mulholland with Bear and Grizz; Novato, CA*

Before training with Vera, we were fearful of potential disastrous consequences of our Fox Terrier's aggression. Sadie's talent and ability were immediately apparent when we followed Vera's instructions! Our very energetic terrier is now a delight to have in the family and great fun to take through the agility obstacle course.

— *Katherine Maxwell with Sadie; Novato, CA*

My young Boxer, Spock, was very aggressive and unmanageable. Even after hiring several so-called dog trainers, Spock continued to get worse. When I came to Vera I was at the end of my rope. Her skill and compassion for dogs were immediately apparent. When Vera works with a dog she moves like a fish in the water. The dogs adore her. Today Spock is a confident, obedient and easygoing dog. What a difference the right trainer makes!

— *Chantal Philipona Young*
with Spock and Guinan; Tiburon, CA

Vera, the ultimate intellectual alpha dog, has made dog training into a science that she can actually teach you. Owning a dog becomes a joy and not a chore.

— *Jane Norman with Noodles; Novato, CA*

Although we went to basic dog training with our very sensitive but aggressive Shepherd, we were not able to control Tenya's behavior. Vera taught us how to train Tenya. She saved Tenya from a life where she would be relegated to the house and yard, because we would not have been able to take her anywhere. I would give Vera three thumbs up, but I only have two!

— *Al Cornwell with Tenya; Novato, CA*

Words fail to express my gratitude for what Vera has taught both my German Shepherd Dog, Pele, and me. Some images will be forever lasered into my mind's eye — and lessons I've learned from her have also transferred into my personal life.

— *Karen Bierer with Pele; Mill Valley, CA*

Barking Up the Right Tree

Barking Up the Right Tree

Tales Out of Dog School

Vera Reeves

21st-Century Publishing
Henderson, Nevada

All training situations are real. In order to protect the privacy of individuals — human and canine — the names are imaginary and the characters and events have been synthesized, so that any resemblance to actual persons or dogs is purely coincidental. This is not a work of fiction.

Published by 21st-Century Publishing
Address: 16 W. Pacific Ave. #3, Henderson, NV 89015
Phone: 702/564-1665
Websites: www.21st-centurypublishing.com
          www.barking-up-the-right-tree.com

This book may also be purchased by calling Atherton Acres Kennels at 415/897-7311.

Cover photo of Vera Reeves and her
Riesenschnauzer "Hexer von Elberfeld"
© by Brad Mangin

Also by Vera Reeves:
Bark and Bite: Applied Ethology in Dog Training

Contents

Acknowledgements

My deep gratitude to Betty Evans for her generous support of this book, as well as for the endless hours in which we explored canine behavior and training theories and practices. Special thanks to Robert Vance, co-founder of the original San Francisco Police Canine Unit and owner of the American Canine Institute, for taking me under his wing when I was a young dog trainer and for sharing his profound knowledge and experience freely. Special thanks also to Hans-Jurgen Freitag, whom I consider one of the best dog trainers in the world, for his ongoing support. The dynamic exchange of ideas and methods with other accomplished trainers is the lifeblood of effective and humane training. Thank you to my many teachers, colleagues and training friends who have enriched me more than they will ever know. There are so many that I could fill pages with their names. But two stand out: Sapir Weiss and Jan Ilkiw.

My very special thanks to John Grissim for putting the idea of this book into my head and for his advice and caring. Thank you to the many people who helped bring this book to fruition: Patricia Morgan and Jennifer Klein for first edits, my agent Amy Rennert, Louise Kollenbaum, my publisher Deke Castleman, my copy editor Candace Hogan and Katherine Maxwell and Bob Hitchman. Thank you to my clients whose desire to improve their relationships with their dogs has led them to me.

And last but not least, I thank my mother for having instilled and nurtured in me a love of nature and a passion for animals.

Foreword

A dog who has no possibility to learn and give complete expression to his innate abilities degenerates in spirit, withers emotionally and is a pitiful creature.
— *Eberhard Trumler*

Most people get dogs out of a desire to have a profound rapport with an animal. But often the communication between human and dog goes wide of the mark and the needs of neither are met. It is difficult for many dog owners to find support for building a satisfying connection with their dogs, because this advice is not generally given in obedience courses that merely teach how to bribe or intimidate dogs into occasional compliance.

For me, dog training is less about teaching simple skills than it is about repairing the fabric of the relationship between dogs and their people. *Barking Up the Right Tree* is a book about the extraordinary close companionship we humans can build with our remarkably adaptive and gifted dogs if we learn to understand their innate program. To our good fortune, this program is very user-friendly! Instead of working against, we work with our dogs' talents and forge a bond that is as expressive and enduring as any tie on this Earth can ever be.

Prologue

In the Whelping Box

The sound of a slight groan jolts me fully into consciousness. It is long past midnight and I must have succumbed to sleep despite my resolve to be at the ready for Ilka's first birth. A splendid canine midwife I turned out to be!

Ilka is my black Riesenschnauzer[1] bitch. Having foreseen her need for security and quietude, I had converted my study into a nursery, a sizable whelping box in the middle, and the requisite paraphernalia—baby scale, disinfectant, hospital tape, scissors, weight and temperature charts, heat lamp, towels, stacks of old newspapers, stethoscope, and perhaps most importantly, Ilka's veterinarian's home phone number in easy reach. Ilka seemed to approve of the accommodations and had settled into the whelping box with obvious satisfaction.

With said groan, Ilka unceremoniously plops her first puppy. While I fumble for scissors to cut the umbilical cord and for towels to rub the puppy dry and to further circulation and breathing, Ilka has peeled her offspring out of its umbilical sac, severed the umbilical cord with her teeth, and is licking the puppy vigorously but gently. Under this maternal attention the tiny creature opens his little mouth widely, sticks out his pink tongue and lets out his first breath,

[1]The German Riesenschnauzer is the progenitor of the American Giant Schnauzer, whom he vaguely resembles. There are, however, such significant differences in breeding requirements, hair-coat, structure and temperament between the two strains that they have become de facto different breeds.

1

accompanied by a little scream. Ilka continues to lick her newborn son, to dry him and to clean off all residue of blood and mucus. The puppy has other plans. He wiggles and squirms vigorously like a huge black mole. As soon as he can escape—although born blind, deaf, and with an undeveloped sense of smell—he crawls with great determination toward Ilka's belly and immediately latches onto one of her nipples. His little paws massage his mother's teats and the noisy smacking sounds prove that his maiden quest for nourishment is being crowned by success. When he becomes a young dog, this massaging movement of the puppy's paws will turn into Giving the Paw, an appeasement and bonding behavior.

Twenty minutes later, Ilka stands up again and drops puppy number two. Number one is not done drinking yet; he hangs on his mother's teat like a big black suction cup. This delights me, because it is clearly a sign of strength and vitality. While Ilka sets to work on her second pup, I seize the opportunity to record the first one's weight and sex and equip him with a loose-fitting hospital band rather unimaginatively marked "One." My responsibilities have been very quickly reduced from midwifely duties to performing menial labor.

How is it possible that Ilka knows so much about birthing and, as we shall see later, about raising and teaching her brood? We humans read books on giving birth. We take classes and choose between natural, semi-natural and supposedly dreadful civilized ways of giving birth. And it only starts there. Mountains of books exist on how to raise children. And when we have educated ourselves, sometimes even beyond our capacity to comprehend, we choose what we consider the right approach. In spite of the conscious choice we make, we are plagued by constant doubts, never really sure that we should not set up a therapy fund for our children along with saving money for their college tuition.

Prologue

Animals, even higher animals like our dogs, cannot make such choices. Much of their behavior is predetermined and cannot be significantly altered. These inborn motor patterns have effectively evolved to ensure survival of the individual and the species. In nature, abnormal inherited conduct is usually not passed on. A dog mother who is inept during birthing or so disturbed or careless that she damages or kills her offspring, luckily for the species, cannot pass on her genes. Dogs who are too inept to hunt or too shy to scavenge, or who egregiously cross the boundaries of accepted social manner in the canine pack, cannot procreate, because anti-social or otherwise dysfunctional behavior results in their being ostracized or killed. (With domestic dogs, however, greedy or incompetent breeders often continue to use such mentally disturbed animals as breeding stock. They take the puppies away from murderous bitches and raise them by hand, thereby passing on what can only be called mental illness. But that is another soapbox.)

At dawn five black little creatures, two males and three females, more resembling moles than dogs, are huddled by their mother's belly. In only a few weeks their tiny round bodies will be muscled and lean and they will run as fast as the wind. They will wrestle and tumble, hunt for mice and tennis balls and steal each other's toys. But for now, in their dark and soundless world, all they really need to know for survival is that warmth and a full belly mean contentment and security.

For the next few days, except to relieve herself, Ilka does not want to leave the whelping box. Her almost constant ministrations to her puppies' welfare—keeping them fed, warm and clean—are interrupted only by my meddling. I weigh the pups and chart their progress. Daily their numbered hospital bands are exchanged for larger ones. Ilka al-

3

lows me to handle her puppies, but she keeps a sharp eye on my activities.

For a time, I have taken it upon myself to fulfill the part that nature has determined for the father. He guards the den, keeps the other members of the group away and procures nourishment for the bitch and her pups. That is an easy enough job, I think. Instead of hunting mice and rabbits and digging up diverse roots or raiding compost heaps and garbage dumps and regurgitating half-digested food for the mother, I simply go to the refrigerator, chop up some beef heart or kidneys, add some brown rice and carrots for good measure, drop them in a bowl and serve the stuff to Ilka. She pays no mind that I did not first regurgitate this culinary delight and gobbles it down. Guarding the lair is also not difficult. I simply keep the door to the "den" closed and shoo the other dogs away when they crowd curiously outside the door. However, if I don't soon extend my hunting forays to the grocery store, the specter of famine looms. Furthermore, perhaps because I am of Teutonic extraction, I believe in the restorative powers of a cool beer, particularly on a hot summer day. Therefore, running out of beer is a crisis not to be underestimated. The door to the den is safely locked, not just closed. The puppies and mother are resting comfortably. Congratulating myself on my circumspection, I set out to attend to the momentous requirements of life.

These requirements do not entirely consist of stocking the larder and refrigerator with refreshing brews, however. With my partner Betty, I own and run a boarding and training kennel, Atherton Acres, in Marin County in the San Francisco North Bay Area. While Betty supervises the day-to-day boarding proceedings, I am in charge of the training program. But since it is a small kennel, both of us have to assume the role of jack-of-all-trades at times.

Prologue

My love of dogs and horses was practically sucked in with mother's milk. I grew up in Germany with Riesenschnauzers and much of my free time was spent with them or at the riding stable. At least one of my dogs accompanied me almost everywhere, to Girl Scout sessions and excursions when I was a child and smuggled into lectures at the university when I was an adult. At the age of fifteen I took over the responsibility of schooling and competing with our dogs in working dog trials, for the first ten years under the watchful eyes of highly accomplished instructors.

After I finished university with a double major in English and German Literature, it dawned on me, somewhat belatedly, that the last thing I wanted to do was to teach those subjects. Through previous visits to the United States, I had already learned of the dearth of competent accessible dog training in this part of the world. So I packed my bags, and full of entrepreneurial spirit, sailed across the ocean on the QE 2 with my Riesenschnauzer, Bautzi, and established a dog-training school in the San Francisco Bay Area where I had friends. Some ten years later, I teamed up with Betty, a lapsed geneticist, who always wanted to work with dogs, and we bought Atherton Acres together.

When I return from my brief absence and enter the den the room is empty. A fine guardian I am! I know some mentally disturbed bitches kill their young and sometimes even eat them, but surely not Ilka! But what if she clumsily crushed them by rolling over? Not a peep, no sign of little black bodies mangled, nothing. Oh God! Probably something dreadful happened. Fighting down my mounting panic, I now glimpse the door to the yard being slightly ajar. As I fly out of the nursery, I can faintly hear the puppies' ululations. They are alive, at least! My prayer of thanks is necessarily short, because divine inspiration is still absent as to the puppies' exact location. The fenced yard is deserted. There is no sign of Ilka, and the puppies' squeals sound as if someone is roasting them alive. Where oh where are they? I call Ilka without much hope for obedience, given the circumstances. But here she comes, crawling on her belly from a hole under the porch, cobwebs in her beard and on her ears and gray with dust and sand. I peek under the porch; the pups seem hale and hearty, but restless and clearly disconcerted about having to go slumming in a dank hole in the ground. And they cannot even crawl away. At this tender age, all normal puppies crawl more or less in circles, another wise provision of nature, as it is not always easy for a canine mother to keep a large litter of vital pups in the lair.

Ilka is delighted to see me, but patently upset about her puppies' discomfort. The wailing of a pup automatically initiates a mother's nurturing and protective responses. Ilka is caught in a conflict of two courses of action: to make the puppies comfortable so they don't cry and to keep them safe. She is unable to deal constructively with the fact that her very idea of safety created this puppy rebellion. Ilka now displays stereotypical conflict behavior. She paces and whines, sits down and yawns, shakes, relieves herself (which is inappropriate, under the circumstances) and appears totally beside herself. She worms her way back under the porch and attempts to nurse and appease her offspring once more, to no avail.

What choice do I have? Spiders are not my friends, but using rather impious language under my breath, I wriggle headfirst through the small aperture under the porch and retrieve the squeaking critters one by one. Their normally sleek black coats are encrusted with dust and debris. They look like they have been breaded for frying, five to a pan. Come to think of it, I must have had a similarly indecorous appearance. The puppies are exhausted from voicing their protest and instantly huddle together and go to sleep. As Ilka resumes her place in the whelping box, she appears thoroughly relieved that the dilemma is solved. The puppies are content, and watchdog Vera is back on duty.

Nevertheless, over the next several days, she stuffs her hapless offspring under the porch a few more times while I'm gone. She has resolved her quandary in favor of the stronger genetic program, namely, safety before comfort. Free choice had nothing to do with her decision. She has now added experience to her inborn nurturing proficiency by learning that her puppies are not in mortal danger every time they squeak. The puppies loathe it; Ilka, however, clearly thinks, or I should say more correctly is predestined to feel, that this is safer than the whelping box, where she can hear the other dogs snuffling curiously behind the door. There is no way I can explain to her that the door is locked and the other dogs cannot open it. Nor can I reprimand her. I would only intensify her inner turmoil by adding my hostility or displeasure into the cauldron of confusion. Ilka's hiding of her puppies ends only when they are old enough, after about twelve days, to be visited by some of the other dogs in her presence. Once she has transcended her predetermined skill of protecting and nurturing her progeny by learning that her canine pack-mates mean her puppies no harm, the daily excursions under the porch stop. By then I am on intimate terms with all the spiders under the porch.

The puppies are now over three weeks old; their eyes are open but still unfocused and they can hear. At this age the first social contacts are formed; they begin to lick and gnaw at each other with abandon. Their licking and poking at Ilka's mouth has an interesting effect: Ilka regurgitates her half-digested food for her puppies. A motor pattern that may be partly innate and partly accidental now becomes intentional and imprinted in the puppies' brain: Poking at the mouth produces food. Even when the puppies are older and Ilka refuses to regurgitate food for them, this "snout thrust" remains active as a means to effectively appease and bond with their elders. Throughout the dogs' lives they will try to mollify their canine or human superiors by licking and poking at their faces. Although the puppies do not yet leave the whelping box on their own, without fail they crawl to its farthest corner to defecate, a sure sign that their instinctive sense of cleanliness is beginning to develop.

At five weeks of age, the puppies' numbers have been replaced by names. Ammo and Argus for the males, and Apache, Arriba and Amsel for the females. Their overriding motivation, aside from eating, is curiosity. Anything that can be reached can also be chewed! More and more, Ilka growls when the puppies try to nurse; their sharp little teeth must hurt her teats quite a bit. The formerly quiet nursery has been expanded onto the deck and is hopping with activity. The sleep periods become increasingly shorter and when they are not eating or sleeping, the puppies play. And how they play! They wrestle with a great deal of growling and biting; they carry toys around and guard them fiercely from potential thieves; they play dog in the manger and let no one in or out of the door; they chase moving objects, then tackle them with great fanfare; they ambush each other and play tug-of-war. In fact, *all* dog games are, in their nature, either fighting or hunting games. Human visitors are greeted with an overwhelming onslaught of puppy energy and being petted is fine, but untying shoelaces and attacking trouser legs are even better.

Now there are daily excursions to the training field and the adjoining marshes where the puppies can hunt frogs and bugs when they are not wrestling with each other. I feel like

Prologue

the pied piper with the Schnauzer family in tow. My German Shepherd, Falko, had taken it upon himself to assume the duties of ersatz-father. I am thrilled by this development, because his stable disposition and great self-confidence match that of the mother. I never expose my puppies to shy or skittish dogs, let alone cranky ones (or to people of the same characteristics, for that matter). The puppies are to learn that the world is a safe place and that they can trust the judgment of their elders. The little darlings maul their "father" and are even allowed to take food and toys away from him with impunity. He is tolerant, but never loses control of the situation. The puppies adore him and follow him around with a quasi hero-worship.

By the time the puppies are eight weeks old they run fast and bite hard. They run so fast that only another puppy can catch them. I surely can't, particularly when they all scatter to the four winds. However, it is not necessary to exert myself in this most unproductive manner, dashing about with a red face, clasping recalcitrant little bodies into my arms. All I have to do is whistle or call out to them and all the puppies gallop to me as fast as their fat little legs can carry them. When they arrive they spill into my lap, and their expectations of play and a tidbit are never disappointed. They bite so hard that even the ever-tolerant Falko sometimes has to put a stop to it. How does he do this? He simply plays harder than the puppies can comfortably endure. There is no display of anger; if a warning growl is ignored, almost with a grin on his face he pushes the juvenile offender's head to the ground and holds him there for a split second, or simply snatches him by the scruff of the neck and pinches him hard. The little culprit is overwhelmed and a bit cowed, though never terrified or even seriously frightened. But the message is not lost on the young fellow: Don't ever forget that I am in charge! The puppy instinctively responds by lowering his head or jumping up and licking Falko's mouth and sometimes rolling over briefly as a submissive gesture. These submissive gestures, in turn, cause Falko to cease any disciplinary action and the play is resumed as if nothing had happened, except that the little sinner is now a bit more polite.

I don't know what moronic individual was the first to pervert the stereotypical punishing move of pushing a puppy's head down and pinching him in the scruff of the neck into the so-called alpha-roll. The puppy or young dog is shaken by the neck and rolled on his back, usually with the concomitant hysterical exclamations of "NononoNO!!" Generations of featherbrained dog trainers have propagated this cruel and inappropriate technique. Thousands of puppies have been put in fear for their lives at the hands of those who had neither the knowledge nor the compassion to train dogs.

Normal dogs (and knowledgeable humans) proceed as described above: The pinch at the scruff of the neck and the pushing down of the head are quick as lightning and occur without visible buildup of anger, often in the course of rough play. In no way does the elder dog ever shake the puppy like a wet rag or roll him over on his back. The puppy may roll over briefly as a submissive gesture. If at all, this type of punishing is not imparted often by the young dog's elders, because the offender learns very quickly to be more respectful. The dog, as predator, is endowed with an instinctive, stereotypical motor pattern called the "shaking-to-death-reflex." It is designed to suffocate or break the neck of small prey. This movement, as any thinking person would acknowledge, has nothing whatsoever to do with disciplining young dogs.

Ilka has still another way of instilling respect and ensuring her leadership. When she feels her puppies become too bold and disobedient, she herds them all into an open closet or into a corner and refuses to let them leave. The poor fool who defies her is immediately snatched and dragged back and deposited rather roughly. Again, this maneuver is accomplished without anger, almost in the form of a game. When all the puppies acquiesce and sit there looking up at their mother like an obedient kindergarten class, she trots away with a self-satisfied air.

Toys and other objects that serve as prey-substitutes are now beginning to play a bigger part in the puppies' lives. Only a couple of weeks ago their attention shifted in the blink of an eye and rarely did they even carry the same object across the room without getting sidetracked and picking up something else. Stealing toys from siblings by cunning or simple strength is now elevated to an art form. All toys increase dramatically in value when someone else covets them! The little thief often parades his booty in front of the other puppies, in order to incite their envy. After all, what fun is a successful caper when no one admires your cleverness? The burden of ownership can lead to intricate, albeit not always singularly successful, ploys to cache the coveted treasure somewhere safe.

I call the puppies for their dinner. Eating is a favorite activity and four puppies immediately crowd around the little trough and gobble their gruel. Ammo, the greediest of them all, is standing back looking apprehensive. A piece of cardboard protrudes from his little mouth and he is in a quandary how to resolve his dilemma. If he leaves the cardboard behind, by doggie-law, he forfeits ownership. Devouring it would take some time and there is the heavenly delicious gruel calling to him. He is crying piteously, seeming to say with Goethe's Faust, "Two souls, alas, dwell in my breast."

Barking Up the Right Tree

What to do, oh what to do? Hide it! That's what! The unfolding scene fascinates me. Ammo scratches at the linoleum floor with both paws in a digging motion. He then places his precious piece of cardboard into the imaginary hole and pushes his nose along the floor as if he were moving dirt to cover it. Mission accomplished! Without a backward glance Ammo joins the feast.

Hiding an object by burying it is evidently an inherited skill. It is interesting, however, that such actions are exhibited *even if they make no sense under the circumstances*. The dog simply has no choice. A few weeks later Ammo is put in a similar situation in the garden. This time he successfully buries his piece of cardboard in the dirt. From then on he knows the difference and will never again try to bury something in hard ground. Learning now augments the fixed behavior pattern.

The stronger and the more rigid the inborn behavior, the less choice the animal has. Human intelligence and the resulting choices we have are only possible because of the absence of very strong immutable motor patterns. In areas where humans do have strong direct responses, as for instance in many survival situations, conscious choice is superseded by automatic action. However, absence of instinctive behavior is merely a prerequisite for intelligence, not intelligence itself. To classify dogs or dog breeds in terms of their "intelligence," as has been attempted in popular dog literature, flies in the face of any scientific study of animal behavior. In reality, what, how much and how fast a dog can learn is very strongly influenced by the intensity and constellation of his inherited motor patterns.

The puppies without their mother now mingle freely with the rest of the pack, which consists of Schnupp, the Dobermann, and Ben, Grendel and Gandhi, the German

12

Prologue

Shepherds. Ilka does not get along particularly well with the two bitches, Schnupp and Grendel, which is a polite way of saying they would kill each other given half a chance. Nonetheless, all the adult dogs are very lenient with the puppies; this is normal behavior. Grendel, the German Shepherd bitch, likes them well enough, but makes no effort at bonding more than superficially; after all, they are not her children. She is, however, exceedingly tolerant. When the little hellions try to engage her in a game of roughhousing and wrestling, Grendel often simply turns away. This is an unmistakable signal that the puppies understand very well. They then move on to share their puppy joie de vivre with a more welcoming beneficiary. Schnupp, the Dobermann bitch, also does not feel particularly maternal, but likes to play with them, as long as they don't purloin her toys. If a puppy has the effrontery to try, Schnupp strikes at him with the lightning speed of a cobra and pinches him. Everyone knows that a Dobermann's toys are sacred and must not be touched! Once she abandons her toy, however, in order to pursue some other activity, it can be safely picked up by the diminutive hunter and gatherer. Clearly, ownership among dogs is enforced only when the coveted object is in the defender's direct possession. Like a maiden aunt, poor Gandhi is often completely overwhelmed when the puppy-pack mobs him and flees to puppy-safe environs. Ben is friendly, but also forges no particular bond with the Riesenschnauzer pups.

Falko, on the other hand, is now an old hand at this father business. I could watch for hours while he encourages the puppies to develop their skills. During their wrestling games he sets very clear rules of conduct. The puppies must learn not to damage each other or the adults when they play-fight. This lesson will be imprinted into the puppies' brains as bite inhibition. (Although, when they gnaw on much more sensitive human skin with their needle-sharp puppy teeth, it can still be rather irksome.) Father now also plays the role of large prey and invites the puppy-pack to chase and tackle him. One puppy latches onto his ruff, the other snaps brazenly at his hocks, another desperately tries not to be shaken off Falko's bushy tail, and a singularly clever one attempts to cut him off from the flank. Falko is putting on a great show. He collapses and rolls on his side. Now all the puppies are on him like fleshy black leeches. One particularly foolhardy little hunter bites his ear. This is too much! Falko leaps up with a menacing roar and shakes himself vigorously. The puppies are hurled in all directions like rag dolls. Gulliver and the Lilliputians. For a moment, the puppies are awed by this terrible show of strength. However, presently the hunting game resumes.

In addition to trips to the open space, from age five or six weeks on, I often take one puppy at a time downtown to the bank and the hardware store, where it can be exposed to all manners of loud noises and meet lots of people, as well as learn to be away from the family for short periods of time.

The twelfth week, when they will go to their new homes, draws inexorably near. By this time their basic socialization period is nearly concluded. The window for further socialization and exposure stays open for another four weeks and then closes irrevocably. Experiences good and bad are now imprinted, hardwired into the brain. Deficiencies in proper socialization with dogs and humans during this time, as well as disturbed or absent inherited behavior patterns, can never be neutralized. For this reason it is always better to obtain a puppy from a knowledgeable amateur (meaning someone who loves what s/he does) than from a puppy mill or someone for whom breeding dogs is primarily a financial investment. Obtaining a puppy, for instance, whose mother rejected it or that was raised without proper care or proper socialization is always an additional burden on the new owner and will remain so for the rest of the dog's life.

Although Ilka is now less and less concerned with her pups, I dread the thought of having to say good-bye. Ilka's degree of detachment seems in inverse proportion to my becoming bonded to the Schnauzerkinder as they are now called. They trust me unquestionably and I have learned to predict every move they make; I could tell them apart blind-folded, with my hands tied behind my back, as the saying goes, by the way they greet me, their sounds and their way of moving. Argus, who can sit and stare into my eyes for a long time. Apache, the master thief, who always scrambles up my body and gnaws more or less gently on my chin. Ammo, the big boy with the explosive temper, constantly underfoot somehow, forever waiting for me to acknowledge him before he hurtles off with his brother and sisters. Feisty Amsel, who misses nothing, always the first in a scrap. Arriba, the little gangbuster, radiating self-confidence and determi-nation so like her mother. Alas, I can hardly do justice to five puppies at a time. So I resolve to keep Ammo and Apache.

She Was Such
a Cute Puppy

In my experience, well-adjusted, properly socialized, and therefore obedient dogs are almost never given up for adoption. It usually takes a lot of patience, knowledge and willingness to accept the dog's emerging personality in order to rehabilitate a discarded dog. While I disapprove of the easy solution of dumping a dog, there is no doubt that many dogs are better off in their new homes if they are fortunate enough to find an owner who makes a commitment.

"If you don't take Jody and train her, I'm going to have to take her to the pound," says my riding instructor with an air of finality. "She chases horses, livestock, fence fights with the neighbor's dogs, or ducks through a tiny hole in the fence and harasses the neighbor's chickens."

The culprit a young, rather plain looking black and brown Dobermann bitch of about nine months, seems unperturbed about these dire pronouncements. She is fervidly excavating a subterranean tunnel in the horse pasture, ostensibly to go where her owner has sent her many times.

"And will you look at that," Nadia continues, pointing an accusing finger at the dog whose body has all but disappeared in the pit. "I can't have these craters everywhere. Not with horses around. And of course she doesn't listen at all."

"Why don't you keep her in the house when you can't watch her?" I ask, ever so sensibly.

"Impossible!" Nadia flares up. "The minute she is in the

house, all she does is torment Freddy. She carries him around like a stuffed toy and he screams his head off. But she doesn't care. She used to be *so* cute when she was little. She would sit on our laps and cuddle, but she's too big for that now."

"Freddy, that malicious snappish little Pekinese mix?" I ask, not very respectfully. "She *carries* him? It's hard to imagine that Freddy wouldn't fight back. He bites at the slightest provocation."

"I'll show you," Nadia says. "It's time for a break anyway."

Jody follows us into the house and immediately ferrets out Freddy, who is desperately attempting to scurry away. She eagerly snatches him by his plumed tail and picks him up. With great glee and obviously no intention of hurting the little fluff ball, she now carries him upstairs, blithely ignoring that Freddy's head is banging into the stairs with every step she takes. The little dog is screeching his furious objection to his opprobrium.

"You see?" Nadia chuckles, almost against her will. "It may be funny, but poor Freddy already has a bad back!"

There is no doubt that the young Dobermann is quite a nuisance, although I find her infinitely more endearing than that malevolent furry little devil, Freddy. Nevertheless, I certainly don't want to take her home and live with her.

"Why don't you get rid of nasty Freddy, and I could teach you to train Jody?" I offer hopefully.

"Look, Vera, I'm training horses all day long; I don't want to have to train a dog in the evening. Besides, I've gotten rather fond of Freddy. At least I can control him," Nadia shrugs. "You should take Jody. You're between dogs anyway, and you need a project."

I am indeed between dogs. My old Bautzi had died a few months ago at the ripe old age of fourteen and a half, and I am not ready for a new puppy yet. (Bautzi, a pepper-salt Riesenschnauzer, immigrated with me to the United States. She preceded Ilka, Apache and Ammo.)

"If you don't take her, she goes to the pound; they'll find her a home!"

Sure, I think to myself, who would want to keep this nut of a dog? Aloud I say, "Okay, I'll take her. But only until she is trained!"

In contrast to most people who decide to take in a pre-owned dog, I have many years of experience in ameliorating problem behavior in dogs, as well as a fair notion of how the young Dobermann was raised and where the problems lie. Having observed her for more than four months, I had come to know her as an adequately confident and stable dog, who was left to her own devices far too much. In spite of this, the process of rehabilitating this dog turns out to be quite a bit more burdensome than I anticipated.

"I thought you said she was housebroken."

"Well, she is, or at least she was," Nadia flutes. "We haven't let her in the house in months. She's used to being out all day long, but she never messes in her crate at night."

Whatever this dog is, it does not meet my definition of *housebroken*. Jody neither lets me know when she has to go outside, nor does she use the dog door, even after she has been shown. She never ventures into the yard, unless I put her on a leash and drag her out. Immediately she comes back in through the dog door. Clearly, she wants to avoid, to the best of her little Dobermann brain's ability, being put out and left there. She evidently likes the house and moves off the couch only to eat or to go the bathroom. I call her the Couch Barnacle.

Over time I learn to read the minute signal she gives when she has to relieve herself and I try to anticipate her need. Still, I have to be gone sometimes. Nevertheless, I take comfort in the conviction that Jody is really a clean dog at heart. She deposits her piles and puddles right in front of the sliding glass-door to the yard, as far away from the living space as possible!

Several times a day I put her outside with food and let her find her way back in. After some weeks she grasps that she can come back in whenever she wants, and—from one day to the next—she decides to use the dog door in both directions or lets me know that she has to go outside.

My fear that Jody would torment my cat, Buster, by attempting to carry him around like she did Freddy proved groundless. Buster is a large, muscular dark gray tabby who carries himself with the hauteur befitting his statuesque physique. Indeed, Buster and Jody become fast friends. They take their frequent naps together and Jody is allowed to use Buster as a pillow.

On walks Jody learns to come on command very quickly, primarily because she has a voracious appetite. In spite of this, she stays aloof; there is no real sign of bonding to me more than superficially. She is mildly pleased when I come home, but I miss the onslaught of happiness I normally get from dogs I have raised myself. Her ears stay permanently glued back to her head, although she is not submissive.

I am used to living with dogs who speak to me, with their eyes and facial expressions, with their bodies and their voices, and my dogs have learned at an early age to understand my language, not so much the words as the intentions behind the words that are expressed in tone of voice and body language. They learn to accept me as a benevolent and just god and it is easy to maintain a dialogue. (When I was a child my mother told me, "You can read in your dog's eyes if you are his god or his demon." I have never forgotten.)

She Was Such a Cute Puppy

Maintaining easy communication with a dog in a variety of social settings is the true nature of socialization. We don't socialize children by merely letting them play with other children. The child must be guided at an early age to fit into a variety of social structures, be trusting and act appropriately, at least most of the time. Likewise, a young dog must learn to trust and accept benign leadership. A poorly socialized dog cannot bond more than superficially.

While Jody is not exactly disobedient — I am neither god nor demon to her — there simply is no connection between us. She lies on the couch, usually with Buster, and observes the goings on with a stony face. Frequently I find her staring at me, but there is no emotion in her gaze, except maybe a slight bewilderment. It is not even possible to play with Jody. In spite of her highly developed predatory behavior, she has no interest in toys or games, because she has not been properly conditioned. With months of work, this could be overcome, but I have no intention of keeping this peculiar dog that long. All the behaviors I take for granted when I raise a dog from puppyhood are deplorably absent.

When I take her to the beach I get another unpleasant surprise. A surfer in a black wetsuit, surfboard under his arm, etched sharply against the bright sky, comes toward us, and Jody charges what must look to her like an otherworldly monster. She responds to my calling her, but now I have another problem to solve.

I hate making this phone call. "Nadia, Jody is too much dog for you. I don't think she is ever going to be the mild-mannered dog you want. She has loads of prey-drive and a fair amount of aggression that needs to be channeled into proper outlets. She does have to be constantly supervised in order not to get into trouble. You would never be able to let her run around on the ranch. She would terrorize all your students."

Barking Up the Right Tree

"What do you suggest? I'd certainly rather not take her to the pound," Nadia sighs.

Against better judgment I say through only slightly clenched teeth, "I'll buy her from you. I suppose I can train her up and sell her."

"I'll *give* her to you, but you'll end up keeping her!" Nadia augurs.

"No way! She's not my kind of dog. She doesn't even have a beard!"

A few weeks later, I take Jody with me to my riding lesson. She shows no sign of being particularly pleased to be back at her old home. During my lesson she lies stone still under a tree by the riding arena.

"You did a great job training her," Nadia commends me.

"I haven't trained her to stay at all." I am baffled. "Maybe she's not feeling well."

When we go into the house for some coffee, Jody lies by my saddle and my riding boots and waits for my return. As soon as I shoulder my saddle she snatches one boot, races to my car and leaps through the open window. There is no doubt that she does not want to be left behind.

Of course, Nadia was right. I have no talent to be a dog broker. Jody's name was changed to Schnupp, after the first registered Dobermann bitch. Once Little Miss Schnupp, as she came to be called, recognized that she had a permanent home with me, she opened up and became quite communicative. I worked her in Search and Rescue training and through Schutzhund progressive degrees. She died at the age of eleven of bone cancer.

Cast Off

Schnupp was of basically very stable disposition and suffered mostly from more or less benign neglect. Adopting a dog, however, who is the victim of clumsy training attempts is quite another story.

"We fell in love with her at first sight," Valerie recalls. "But she is quite unruly and disobedient, and there is no way we can take her off leash."

Derek nods. "Yeah, she's a handful, all right. I think we're getting a bit too old for training her. You did such a good job on our last Shepherd, do you think you'd like to tackle this one?"

Derek and Valerie, both in their late seventies, have brought me Andy, a two-year-old, female, mostly German-Shepherd-and-some-Husky mix. At my first evaluation she seems quite friendly, cheerfully independent and self-confident.

Ordinarily, I do not like to take dogs for training. It is a foregone conclusion that the dog will obey me, but not necessarily the owner. Although Valerie and Derek are still rather fit, they are physically incapable of training a strong, boisterous dog. Valerie, however, had bred, raised and trained many German Shepherds in her life. Therefore, I have no doubt that she is able to maintain the training.

So it is agreed that I keep Andy as long as necessary, and Derek and Valerie fly back to San Diego where they live. Had I only known what I was in for, Andy would have flown back with them.

Barking Up the Right Tree

The good news is that Andy has impeccable dog-manners. She is not overbearing with more timid dogs and she easily holds her own with the pushy or merely very boisterous ones. She is also fastidiously clean. But what at first glance merely seemed to be her independence turns out to be full-fledged avoidance behavior. Andy, although not timid or submissive, does not trust humans one whit. She is convinced that any but the most superficial interaction with people ends to her detriment. The most innocent request on my part is viewed as a deception. When *she* approaches me out of her free will I can pet her briefly before she saunters off. When *I* call her, however, her immediate reaction is to play keep-away. Although she is fit and trim and a voracious eater, offering her treats does not improve her attitude. She suspects a trap. Getting her to comply with the simplest command is an exercise in self-restraint for the trainer.

Unfortunately, I am all too familiar with the syndrome; I see it at the kennel every day. As soon as Fido hears his name, he runs in the other direction. In Fido's case I simply back him into a corner and put a leash on him in order to deposit him where I want. But Andy has to learn to trust or her behavior will never change. It isn't just a matter of putting a leash on her and forcing her to comply. Clearly, that had been done and not very well. Nor is it a matter of bribing or cajoling her. That, too, had been tried and failed. It is very difficult to clumsily trick a dull dog, but to try this with a dog who learns quickly—and Andy makes associations *very* fast—usually ends in fiasco.

To make matters worse, Andy turns out to be an escape artist extraordinaire. She can squeeze out of the smallest hole and climb the highest fence even if she injures herself in the process. There is no question: If she ever got out she'd head for the wild blue yonder. Our kennel with its fenced exercise areas is set up in such a way that there are always at least two high fences, two gates, two doors, etc., to negotiate before one reaches the real outside. This proves sufficient to prevent her from actually escaping, although one can never be sure to find her where she was left.

The final disaster strikes after we have had Andy for about a month. I get a call from Derek. Valerie has died of a heart attack and could we please find Andy a home. I don't have the heart to abandon her, especially because I know that I *can* change her behavior given enough time, say a year or two. Besides, I'm a sucker for challenges and lost causes. It is a wonder I didn't set out to perform rain dances in the Kalahari Desert.

So Andy comes to live at Atherton Acres Kennels.

First, we have to establish a routine that appears to give Andy a choice in behavior and that frees me or the kennel help from giving her any commands at all. The cooperation of our kennel staff is easily assured.

In the morning she is let out into the exercise area and gets to play with other dogs for about an hour or two. When *I* try to call her inside for her meal she refuses, but when circumstances are set up in such a way that Andy, herself, seems to decide when to return to her run for breakfast, the objective is easily accomplished.

In the evenings, the kennel dogs are locked inside. Most boarders know that they are given a treat and eagerly wait for it by their inside door. Not Andy, of course. She should have no reason to refuse; she likes her run and, once inside, settles down with obvious pleasure on her fur blanket.

"Come in, Andy," I coax.

No way! Andy peeps through the door, ready to bolt.

"Look, I have a cookie."

Andy stares at it with covetous eyes, but does not move.

"Fine. I'm not playing your game." Throwing the cookie on her bed, I leave to attend to the other dogs.

Andy can't stand it. I can hear her sneaking in to eat her treat. When I appear again in the doorway, Andy's face speaks volumes.

I knew it! It was a trap, she seems to think.

"No trap," I answer her. "I just came to bring you another cookie and to straighten your bed." I exit, leaving the door open, and I can practically feel her astonished gaze at my back.

After several more repetitions, Andy tires of the game and awaits me lying contentedly on her bed. She gets a pat and another cookie and I close her in for the night.

It isn't rocket science to outthink even a wily dog, but it does require a lot of forbearance.

It takes about a month to establish a routine and Andy now complies with the requests to go in and out of her run. She still needs a moment to think matters over, however. When called, she runs one extra round in the exercise yard, *then* she comes in. In the evening, she goes in and out once, then settles. This hesitation is not disobedience; it is *conflict behavior.* Just like people vacillating before making a potentially unpleasant phone call, then finally convincing themselves that it couldn't possibly be that bad.

Now I risk taking Andy out into the one-acre training field that is surrounded by a six-foot fence; high, but not insurmountable. Andy checks out the perimeter, but makes no attempt to climb the fence. Apparently, she feels free enough to evade any potential threat or unpleasantness. Every time she scampers by I offer her a treat, which she snatches from my hand before she recoils. When I get bored with this tedious game, I simply leave her to her own devices. As soon as she is good and ready, she comes in for her dinner.

Over the following next months, Andy learns to come when called. She comes on the first call, most of the time, and now enjoys being petted and stroked. I can hug her without her straining to get away. Now I open the fenced marshlands to her and her behavior holds: She comes joyfully when I call her. Whenever she sees me or Betty or any of our kennel staff, she clearly expects good things to happen. Nonetheless, it will be some time before I can actually enforce the recall and make it reliable, because there is still a great danger of a profound setback.

Optimistically, I decide that Andy's training can now continue with a new owner, under my watchful eyes, of course. The word is put out and one day a candidate appears to check out the free dog. In fact, the shoe is on the other foot. The candidate has to meet our standards, and they are high.

I take an instant disliking to her officious comportment. "No way am I giving her Andy!" I sputter.

"Why don't you wait? Maybe she won't even like her," Betty says in her levelheaded way. "I've given the woman some treats to use. Andy and she are both out in the training field; give them some time."

"Yeah, you're right," I concede, although it now seems hard to imagine that anyone would not like Andy. These days, Andy is simply charming. She is playful and quite trusting and just adores being stroked and patted, and she will do just about anything for food.

When I hear Andy's furious barking a surge of apprehension jolts me to my feet. In the eight months we have had her, she has never barked at a person. Grievously flouting the third commandment under my breath, I sprint to the training field.

Andy is barking and nimbly skipping away from the woman who is pursuing, shaking a threatening finger at her, screeching, "Nonono! No bark!"

My blood is up. "Stop that! What the hell do you think you're doing?" I shout.

"I don't want a disobedient dog or one that works only for treats," the woman snaps. "I told her to sit, but she didn't obey. So I pulled her by her collar and tried to push her rear down. And then she just ran away and barked at me," the woman prattles on in the tone of injured feelings I so detest.

There are quite a few zoological appellations I am tempted to hurl at this foolish individual, but I compose myself. "She doesn't owe *you* obedience," I say icily, forcing a polite veneer over my voice. "You're a complete stranger to her. She doesn't have to obey just anyone. You have to *earn* the right to expect obedience from a dog!"

Fortunately, this unpleasant incident does not cause a pronounced relapse in Andy's behavior toward the kennel staff or me. Unfortunately, however, it makes me aware of how tenuous her trust is and how far we still have to go with her. If her new owner were to make any mistakes, her old behavior would quickly surface.

So Andy stays at Atherton Acres.

Even after having prepared Andy for many months now, I see that she is still not ready to confront even the slightest compulsion with equanimity. There is no outright defiance or submission; she simply shuts down and stares at me with wide eyes as if saying, *I knew it!* Just putting her on a leash and collar is stressful for her. I suspect if I gave her just one correction to force obedience, she would stay out of reach again as soon as she was released. So I continue as I have

28

before, working her with positive motivation.

One of our employees to whom Andy has taken a special liking has bought a house and offers to take Andy. Of course, I am elated. Cecilia has been aware of Andy's propensities from the beginning and it is unlikely that she would pressure her unduly. We agree to begin training her with Cecilia in a few weeks, when she has become accustomed to her new home.

At first, Andy seems to settle in well. After a couple of weeks, however, she gravely relapses. She tries to escape from the yard, even when Cecilia is at home. As at the beginning, she does not become submissive, but aloof. I believe Cecilia, who swears she did not pressure Andy.

"It's as if she doesn't like me any more," Cecilia reports, crestfallen.

So Andy returns to Atherton Acres.

Back in her adopted home, Andy once more is the trusting, cheerful dog she has become. She is delighted to see Cecilia and greet all her old friends. For the time being, I forsake all attempts to find her a home or to make her obedience reliable.

The months pass. We have had Andy for almost two years now. Gradually, very gradually, she has learned to tolerate mild forms of compulsion. When I raise my voice to her, she doesn't immediately suspect that worse things are sure to follow. She can now take a snap on the leash in stride. Now I make her recall reliable by compelling her to comply, even if she has other plans, and once again set out to find her a home.

"She's perfect!" I gush to Betty.

Laura and her five-year-old grandson are on the training field, playing with Andy. Not only do Betty and I like Laura at first glance, Andy seems to feel the same way.

So Andy at long last finds a new home. Laura has had her now for almost five years, and Andy is quite obedient and has never once tried to escape. Whenever she comes to the kennel, she is free and open and happy to see all her old friends. Nevertheless, she now considers the kennel accommodations somewhat beneath her and is absolutely thrilled when Laura picks her up to take her home again.

Life With the Schnauzer Family

Cleanliness is Next to Dogliness

I am of the conviction that my sleep is sacred and nothing must interfere with it. Especially in the morning. If I must be awakened from blissful slumber, I wish it to be to the sounds of a babbling brook and singing birds, or perhaps the gentle strains of the second movement of Beethoven's Sixth. However, one of the Schnauzerkinder is whining. Befuddled and without my glasses, I can't even see which one. Better take them both out to do their business. The two of them are sleeping in dog crates in my bedroom. No normal dog wants to soil his own bed. Therefore, they must let me know when they have to go out.

After they have relieved themselves in tandem, I lock them back into their crates and thankfully crawl back under the covers. This does not meet with the little devils' approval. They think five in the morning is a perfectly reasonable time to go and play. I planned ahead the evening before, because in the morning my brain fluids course with the viscosity of cold molasses. By my bed, in easy reach, I deposited a pile of shoes. At the next squeak of Schnauzer origin I hurl a shoe at the crate and roar, "Hush!!" The puppies have no idea from where this projectile is coming, but they learn that squealing without actually having to go out brings on a *very* grumpy Vera who can summon forth loud thunder.

It is not necessary to turn housebreaking into a melodrama, let alone a battle of wills between owner and dog. With the ounce of prevention about which our grandmothers already lectured us, we simply *facilitate* our puppy's cleanliness in the house.

For a couple of months I've been having to let out Ammo and Apache in the early morning, but once I put them back in their crates they are as quiet as little mice and wait to be let out at a more reasonable time. During the day I take them out every few hours and after every nap or meal. If I can't watch them I put them outside in their spacious run. Minor accidents happen infrequently. There are, of course, no emotional outbursts or punishment. I simply invest in a lot of paper towels. From the time they were ten weeks the Schnauzerkinder have used the dog door to go outside for all their major business. By the time Apache and Ammo are five months old they are reliably housebroken, and they mostly sleep through the night.

One notable exception occurs when the Schnauzerkinder are six or seven months old. It is wintertime in California and the rainstorms are strong and frequent. Ammo and Apache, born in the summer, are not used to this. Although getting soaked to the skin while playing in the heaviest downpours or spending hours digging deep, sludgy holes in the marshes and practically marinating in muck and mire are great fun, going out to pee is quite another matter. When I urge them to go out, they stand in the doorway, squinting reluctantly at the wintry gloom, considering if the situation is pressing enough to warrant action. At my insistence, they make a beeline under the overhang and proceed as quickly as possible. Then they rush back into the house and shake themselves as vigorously as if they had become drenched.

Cleanliness is Next to Dogliness

One soggy day, Ammo pokes his head out of the dog door. As the driving rain and wind rip at his beard and eyebrows, he peers disconsolately through half-closed eyes at the sodden yard. How to be a well-behaved, housebroken dog, he seems to think, and not get damp in the process?

Clever Ammo now steps halfway through the dog door, his front feet on the outside, but the business end of him still on the inside. With great contentment on his face, he pees. Unfortunately for him, I happen to be standing right behind him and now propel him outside with my foot. From then on he prefers getting wet to incurring my wrath.

Come and Get It!

🐕 🐕 🐕

With a dog who is properly bonded and trusting, small changes in the owner's approach often bring about remarkable and speedy improvement in the dog's attitude.

"Maaaaggie! Maggie!?? Maggie, COME!"

The boisterous young Kerry-Blue Terrier who indubitably must be Maggie, since there is no other dog within earshot, doesn't give the slightest indication that she recognizes her exasperated owner's adjurations.

Joan, the owner of ostensibly deaf Maggie, gives me a sheepish grin. She is a woman in her fifties, with a good-natured smile and an easygoing demeanor. She came prepared for her first lesson, appropriately clad in jeans and a sweatshirt.

"Maggie does know how to come," Joan declares despite all evidence to the contrary. "Not always, though," she adds needlessly. "When I take her to the park, she comes when she is done playing with the other dogs."

"You mean to say, when she is so tuckered out that she can't play any more?" I ask innocently.

"Something like that," Joan admits vaguely. "She used to come better when she was younger," she sighs. "When there are no dogs to play with, she bothers people. She knows she shouldn't jump, but last week she ran up to a woman sitting on a bench, nursing a baby. The woman was so frightened that she climbed onto the bench and lifted her baby above her head, shrieking. Well, you can imagine Maggie! She thought that was a great game and kept jumping up to

35

see the baby. She wouldn't have hurt it, but it was very embarrassing." Joan hides her face in her hands, but I can see that she is laughing. "That's why I am here," she concludes. "Maggie doesn't listen when she's not on leash!"

Meanwhile, Maggie sniffs and ambles about happily on my one-acre training field. Although escape-proof, this space, together with the adjoining three acres of fenced marshland, is large enough to give dogs the illusion of complete freedom. I ask Joan to approach Maggie and pat her. The Kerry-Blue briefly looks up when Joan comes near and wags her tail noncommittally. She makes no attempt to escape and seems mildly pleased when Joan strokes her. After a moment, she has enough of this demonstration of affection and scampers off.

I am heartened by the fact that Maggie lets her owner approach without seeking to get away, because it proves that the breach of bonding or trust is not too severe. "Let's hide," I suggest. "I want to see if she even notices you're gone." We hide behind one of the blinds on my training field. Maggie is so busy sniffing, she has no idea we have deserted her. After a few moments, however, she senses that something is amiss and begins a somewhat haphazard search. Her lack of success intensifies her efforts. When she finally ferrets us out, her relief is palpable. She hurtles toward Joan, a shaggy black cannonball. Wildly leaping up, she fairly squeals with excitement.

Judging from Maggie's previous behavior, I am certain I can predict the next installment of the scenario. Sure enough.

"No, Maggie! Nononono! No jumping! NO!" Joan's voice rises a perfect fifth with each expostulation, the last No being so high-pitched that only her dog can hear her.

"She knows not to jump," Joan assures me.

I am always a bit amused at all the things owners claim their dogs understand, when there is absolutely no evidence of this. "What else does Maggie know?" I emphasize the last word and make no effort to suppress a smirk.

Fortunately, Joan has a good sense of humor. "Maggie does know how to sit," she asserts with a chuckle. "Shall I show you?" she asks hopefully.

I am not exactly biting my nails in anticipation of a sparkling performance. "By all means, do!" I nod agreeably, suppressing a sigh.

"Maggie!? Sit?" Joan pleads.

Not surprisingly, Maggie looks up and wags her tail, but displays no intention of sitting. Joan now kneels in front of her dog. I am not quite sure if she is genuflecting in prayer for success, begging on bended knee, or perhaps thinking that Maggie is unable to hear if the source of the command is more than three inches from her ears.

"Maggie, sit," she repeats while pulling slightly at Maggie's collar.

Maggie sits.

"Is there hope for us?" Joan asks only half jokingly.

Yes, indeed, there is. Actually, Joan does not have a profound problem with Maggie. Maggie is energetic and playful, open and free in interaction with people, loves to eat, adores chasing tennis balls and, like many terriers, lives for a good game of tug-o'-war. These are all behaviors that are testimony to proper upbringing and are going to aid greatly in training. I ask Joan to leave Maggie with me for half an hour, suggesting she go have a cup of coffee somewhere.

When Joan returns, I have her take a seat at the edge of the training field. I take Maggie into the middle of the field and turn her loose. She frolics for a moment and turns her head to me. I use the opportunity and call her. She races to me and I allow her to jump at me. I roughhouse a bit with her and then throw the tennis ball, which she pursues eagerly. (This, of course is what we were practicing while Joan was gone. Every time Maggie came to me, she expected boisterous playtime or food.) I call her once more and again she shoots towards me immediately.

This is too much for Joan. "I don't believe this. Are you sure this is my dog?" she jokes, patting Maggie, who is now sitting in her lap. "What did I do wrong? I can see you are going to tell me!"

And I do. "Joan, if you encounter an old friend whom you haven't seen in a while, how do you greet him?"

Joan isn't sure where this is going. She glances at me askance as if this were a trick question, which it is. "I'll probably give him a hug," she says, choosing her words with care.

"Right. And if your friend, instead of hugging you back, screams at you or even pushes you away, what then?"

When Joan hesitates, I provide the answer myself. "Not only won't you hug him again, you'll certainly give him a wide berth the next time you meet him, because you think he is not quite right in the head."

Joan sees the logic in this. I explain to her (at some length, I fear) that poking their snout at a superior's face is hardwired bonding and appeasement behavior for young dogs (and those young at heart), just as shaking hands and hugging is for humans. The jumping is only a means of equalizing the difference in height. Repeated rebuffs will stop the dog from jumping; they also will usually extinguish the behavior that leads up to this doggie greeting, namely, the coming to the owner.

"So you see," I conclude my oration, "if owners walked on all fours, their dogs would not have to jump!"

"Well, I don't really mind if she jumps on me," Joan concedes, "but I definitely don't want her to jump at other people."

"Nor should she," I agree. "You get no argument from

me on that issue. Moreover, she should not even be allowed to *approach* other people without your permission. Some people are easily frightened of dogs. Dog owners should have the courtesy to recognize this. Simply shouting that the dog is friendly is not enough."

Now Joan is catching on. "I'll call her away when she starts to run up to someone, and when she comes, I'll let her jump up on me. Is that it?"

"Exactly! You will also find that after a while she'll be less and less inclined to work off her pent-up innate social behavior on strangers."

Joan's assignment for the next couple of weeks consists of rewarding Maggie with several tidbits every time she comes. While Joan does not have to encourage Maggie to jump up, she must not punish her when she does. To minimize the jumping, I advise Joan to bend down to Maggie's level as much as possible. In addition, there is to be some sort of game—tug-o'-war, playing with the tennis ball, or simply a bit of roughhousing—each time Maggie responds to a call. Once she does so reliably, we will work on Heel, Sit, and Down, first on a learn-by-reward basis and, much later, we will compel Maggie to comply even if she has other plans.

A couple of weeks later, Joan, with Maggie leading the way, appears at her lesson with the biggest grin on her face. "I have just got to tell you what happened to us."

I am used to clients who tell me dog stories at epic length. By the time I have politely listened to their wealth of detail, half the lesson is over. In my most pedantic manner I say, "First things first. Tell me how the training with Maggie went. Any problems?"

"No, it's wonderful. She comes every time I call her, even when there are other dogs around." And as if to prove her case, Joan calls Maggie, who is amusing herself at some distance. The Kerry Blue, ears flapping, instantly turns and races to her owner, who praises her profusely and feeds her some treats. "But I really have to tell you our experience," she says excitedly.

At the park, one of Maggie's little canine buddies, a young German Shepherd Dog named Max, would come lickety-split when Joan called Maggie—partly, perhaps, because of the similar-sounding names, but mostly because he knew that treats and a game were in the offing when he heard someone shouting, "Maggie!"

Max does not come to his owner when called, though. Joan, replete with the convert's evangelistic zeal, approached Max's owner with the suggestion that she also try using treats and a game for a reward. Max's owner, however, wanted none of this soft-soap dog training. In her expert opinion, a dog was supposed to come, it was his duty, and rewards—perish the thought—would just spoil the dog into expecting a tidbit every time.

One fine day, as Maggie and Max were playing and Maggie was coming to her owner and Max was not, Max spied something of interest at the other side of the ball field and sped off. Unfortunately, he raced straight to the parking lot and on to the adjoining road. Max's owner called in vain. She now shouted to Joan in desperation: "Call him!! Call him!!"

"So I did, and he came right away. Can you believe it?" Joan concludes her story. "Well, if that doesn't convince her, nothing will," she says screwing her eyes heavenward. "People are so stupid—who would argue with success?" she adds philosophically.

"Actually," I reply, "you are in illustrious company with your frustration. As the poet Schiller says: 'Against stupidity the very Gods themselves contend in vain.'"

Allegro —
ma non troppo

Unfortunately, not all training difficulties are as easily and satisfactorily solved, even if the problem behavior is not very deep-seated.

Mark and Tracy, a young couple, California-tanned and lean and trim in their designer jogging clothes, have brought me their one-year-old yellow Labrador Retriever named Allegro. More aptly, his name should be Larghissimo. He is morbidly obese and looks like a huge potato dumpling with legs. At an age where he should have nearly limitless energy, he can barely run. Whereas Maggie was vivacious and outgoing, Allegro is sulky and reserved, though not hostile. He turns up his nose at offered treats and has no use at all for a ball or any toy. Like Maggie, he doesn't come when he is called, but does not run away when approached, although he shows no signs of excitement when petted. He simply seems to take their affection for granted. He is not hand-shy and evidently was raised in a caring and lenient environment. A lovable lump.

Clearly, to Mark and Tracy the young Lab is the apple of their collective eye. They work at home and someone is always with the dog. When he was a puppy he was reprimanded mildly for jumping up, but as Tracy confides, "He was so happy. And when he's happy, we're happy. So we didn't really correct him. It seemed cruel."

The root of Allegro's lack of compliance is evidently

not inappropriate punishment. He has a somewhat independent nature, but does not like to be left. When we hide in the blind, Allegro lumbers across the training field in a halfhearted attempt to locate his owners. After a few minutes, he is rendered hors de combat and lies down in the shade. Although he continues to look around in case he can catch sight of them, he makes no further endeavors at exerting energy.

Tears well up in Tracy's eyes. "He didn't even really look for us," she states the obvious. "It was probably too hot for him," she consoles herself.

"Tracy and Mark," I begin, having the irrepressible feeling that this job is going to be like digging ditches, "your dog has two problems: Number one, he is so grossly obese that he can hardly move, and number two, you spoil him so much that he wants for nothing. He has to want *something* if you intend to train him with positive motivation. The more he wants something, the faster he learns. The only alternative is force, which—"

"Oh, no! We wouldn't want that," Tracy interrupts. I haven't heard a peep from Mark yet, but he seems to concur.

"Er—right. I was going to say that judicious use of force is only a choice, in my opinion, if the dog thoroughly understands and masters the exercise, when the dog has successfully completed at least fifty repetitions without the trainer pressuring the dog in any way. Then, and only then, we correct the dog when he makes an obviously avoidable mistake."

Tracy looks as relieved as if I had just forgone the decision of singling out Allegro's liver for pate de foie gras. "So what do we do?" she asks quite reasonably.

"You will feed Allegro nothing in a bowl. Nothing! You

cut low-fat turkey franks, turkey meat, or soft meaty doggie treats into dime-sized pieces. You let him know that you have food. When you call him and he comes, you feed him several pieces of meat, each about the size of half a peanut, *one piece at a time* and praise him a lot. Let him think you are a walking vending machine. If he doesn't come, you put the food away and don't try again until the next day. In other words, if he wants to eat he has to come and get it."

"But that's cruel," whines Tracy. Mark says nothing.

I am not known for my saintly patience. "What's cruel is that your dog is so overweight he can barely walk, not to mention run. Dogs are meant to run; their body structure is that of a runner. There is nothing cruel about Allegro having to move his butt to pick up his food from your hand. If he would rather sniff around, he is obviously not hungry. With this method you make him healthy and obedient."

"But we don't want to starve him," Tracy demurs plaintively.

"Starvation has nothing to do with skipping a few meals. By nature, dogs are feast-then-fast animals. Actually, your dog could easily not eat for a month and not be anywhere near starvation." I am not exaggerating.

Tracy looks aghast, as though I had handed her a blindfold and summoned the execution squad.

"You see?" pipes up Mark, unexpectedly, breaking his silence.

I had hardly counted upon support from that quarter, and I flash Mark a conspiratorial grin, not forgetting that Tracy is the one I have to convince.

"Can't I feed him anything else?"

"Carrots," I respond cold-heartedly. "You can feed him an occasional treat of raw carrots or other raw vegetables." Anticipating her objection I continue, "If he does not eat

43

them, he is not hungry enough." I bid them good-bye with my standard, "Come back in a couple of weeks. If you run into a problem, give me a call."

Two weeks later, Tracy and Mark appear with Allegro, who does not seem to have shed an ounce. "He is doing really well," Tracy claims proudly. Mark simply nods, having subsided into his reticence again.

I remain unconvinced. Circumlocution not being one of my strong points, I grumble, "He hasn't lost any weight. Well, let's see how it goes."

Inevitably, there is no improvement in Allegro's obedience. He wanders around, sniffing and completely ignoring his pleading owners' offerings of tasty morsels. Tracy swears on a stack of bibles that Allegro was only fed a few measly crumbs each time he came, which he did much, much better in their yard.

A skeptic at heart, I find it difficult to believe this assertion. But it is not impossible. In some cases weight loss is exceedingly slow in the beginning, when the regimen cannot be supported with increased exercise due to the dog's lack of stamina. Consequently, the dog's food-seeking behavior is not very strong, in any case not strong enough to overcome the distractions of a new place. In familiar surroundings the exercise may well show a certain measure of success.

I send them home with the reiterated salutary advice that the dog must be hungry enough so he would more readily eat than amuse himself elsewhere.

Another two weeks brings only a small change. If the dog has lost weight I can't tell, but he does come two or three times when Tracy calls. After that he is evidently no longer hungry. Subsequent weeks deliver a measurable improvement, as the dog loses a little weight, but by no means a mastering of the exercise. At no point do I think that pressuring Allegro to perform more reliably is justified, because the skill itself is only partially learned. However, the owners appear thrilled.

Well, you can lead the horse to water, but you can't make him drink, as the quaint saying goes. I'm not even above giving the horse a substantial shove. I knew perfectly well that someone was sneaking Allegro extra rations. Perhaps he was provided the food that the owners denied themselves. Allegro came to our kennel to board, heavy as always, and just as slipshod in his obedience. Although I would chalk up Allegro's training as a failure, his owners seemed genuinely satisfied. Apparently, going through the motions of training met their notion of having thrown their sacrifice to the canine gods.

Life With
the Schnauzer Family

Learning Games

Like most puppies, the Schnauzer twins view just about every moving or movable object as a toy. This inborn behavior is hardly surprising in predators. Toys are really just prey-substitutes for them. I am unable and unwilling to bring home half-dead chickens, rabbits or gophers so they can practice and improve their predatory skills, although that course of action would clearly benefit my leather chair, which the little hunters have begun to eviscerate in a moment of my inattention. Although they play with balls and chew toys, they zero in on items of animal origin, like leather, other soft or fuzzy things, even fake fur. Feather dusters are almost as good as chickens, and brooms made of horse hair, particularly when they are being moved in an effort to contain the dog hair on the floor, are especially tempting. Ilka, far from merely observing her remaining brood, actively participates in the hunt. Rather than being aghast, I am delighted by this evidence of strong prey behavior. It is a trait that I can guide to some extent and use effectively in training later on.

I don't want to turn into a raving lunatic by charging about, wresting unapproved toys from uncooperative puppies. In the process I would be undermining any trust I wish to instill in them. Therefore, I take a more effective course of action.

Barking Up the Right Tree

First, I puppy-proof the house. With an experienced eye, I transfer to safer locations anything that could be plundered and destroyed in a heist by the larcenous Schnauzer twins and their colluding mother. I refuse to sit on orange crates; therefore, I plan to replace the leather furniture after the Schnauzerkinder have grown up. It is better to face facts than make myself crazy in a battle no one wins. When I can't watch the thieving trio, I put them outside, saving myself a lot of aggravation.

Should one of them find a forbidden or dangerous toy in spite of my precaution, such as a small rock that can (and will) be swallowed or a piece of metal, or even my favorite shoe, I do not chase the little collector and force him to give up his treasure. This would only teach my puppies to be more sneaky and run away faster the next time. After all, their little Schnauzer brains will never understand that these items are taboo or unsafe. Instead, I feign approval: "Oh, such a clever puppy! You found my shoe (or a rock, or this lovely putrefied bird-mummy) for me! I'll trade you for this cookie." It works because it's a win-win situation. My dogs *never* run away from me, because they expect that there is a good chance that I will buy their booty or at the very least not compete for it. Of course, later, *much* later, the Schnauzerkinder will have to learn that they must relinquish their possession if I demand it. But even then, I use this right very sparingly.

Second, I encourage and develop the puppies' prey behavior and direct it onto approved toys. In this endeavor I work against time. If a dog does not learn to play with balls or certain toys when he is young, he almost never will. This missed opportunity is a terrible loss for the dog.

The Puppy Fishing toy with a soft toy tied to the end of the string is very popular. Playing with two balls keeps and develops the twins' interest more than a single ball would. One ball flies, and the puppy returns to get the second one in my hand. When he drops the first ball, the second one flies into the air. This is an effortless and very fun way to teach him to return with a thrown ball. We also play this same game with sticks and pieces of rubber hose.

Tug-o'-war is also, of course, highly popular. I have cut a leg off my old jeans and tied a knot in it. In the secret language of the family this becomes a knuddel. Knuddels make wonderful cheap tug toys and the knots make them heavy enough to be thrown. Tug-o'-war is a game I always let the puppy win. I make Apache and Ammo progressively put in more effort, but when they do, they are allowed to carry the knuddel around. Usually they bring it back so the game can enter another round.

Ripping and tearing is part of the prey behavior sequence. Cardboard boxes or the cardboard rolls from paper towels work beautifully for this. I remove all tape and staples and let the dogs rip up the carton. Even if they eat the cardboard, it won't harm them.

It seems that the desire to amass riches is not exclusively a human condition. Ammo has learned from experience that prized possessions are best tucked into soft ground. He has found a favorite spot in the front yard, under the plumbagos. Every day he returns from ensconcing a scrap of cardboard, with sticky blue flowers behind his floppy ears and in his beard and an idiotically blissful expression on his face, looking just like a hippie bridegroom.

Nevertheless, when he is out on the training field, playing with the rest of his family, even burying his shred of cardboard does not seem safe enough for Ammo. Once he has dug a deep pit and lowered his toy into its final resting place, he is plagued by the constant worry that canine grave robbers may discover his treasure. Oh, the infernal burden of wealth! He parades around the hidden treasure, worry-wrinkles on his forehead. This worry is entirely of his own making, as none of the other dogs are the least bit interested in his hoard. Every few seconds he reassures himself that his cache is undisturbed, much like a rich man in an unsavory bar, patting his bulging wallet to ascertain that it has not been stolen yet. Inevitably, this draws everybody's attention, including mine. As I amble in the direction of Ammo's treasure trove, he frantically tries to block my approach with his body. He jumps around anxiously, attempting to goad me into playing with him, away, far, far away from his prize possession. I capitulate and withdraw. But Ammo has worked himself into quite a state. Clearly, no one can be trusted! With great haste he unearths his property and once again nervously searches for a hiding place. I am not heartless and therefore let him into the front yard to add his cardboard to his stockpile under the plumbagos. He rejoins the group, visibly relieved, but I could have told him that the dirt on his nose and the flowers in his beard are a dead give-away.

Apache, the master thief, does not generally bury her booty. She packs everything very neatly under a bookshelf with her feet. For months now I have not been able to explain the loss of several knives, spatulas and serving spoons. But one fine day I observe Apache on tiptoe, pilfering utensils out of the sink. She licks them clean and absconds with her loot to add it to her already existing stash. Once I discover her treasure trove, however, she never uses the same location again.

Wrestling and biting are also high on the list of favorite prey games. When I dash through the house to find the ringing telephone, at least one puppy latches onto my pants, and I drag him or her along like a wet rag tied to my leg. Now that they are getting a bit taller, grabbing sweatshirts and particularly my heavy parka is often invitation to play. A Riesenschnauzer is a mouth with a dog attached, sort of like a canine pac-man. To become worried, or worse, hysterical, about this perfectly natural way to play is absurd. On the contrary, like Big Daddy Falko, I use this opportunity to teach the puppies, in a playful non-threatening way that I am *always* stronger. People who were afraid to play with the dog in this way owned some of the nastiest dogs I have known. Their constant anxious clamor of, "No biting!" is very correctly interpreted by the dog as fear of losing control.

Ilka is a mighty mouse hunter. The twins take their mother's example and dig big holes in their pursuit of little mice. I fear for my surviving rosebushes. Schnupp, the Dobermann, the mightiest hunter of them all, has already devastated several of them in her tireless battle against marauding gophers. These gophers are as big and brazen as pit bulls. In her fervor, Schnupp dug craters the size of the one that preceded the extinction of the dinosaurs.

Of course, I must not suppress perfectly natural behavior. If I tried, the dog would pay a heavy price. But I *can* ban the dogs from my rose garden by not letting them play in that area. When I cannot supervise them, they are not allowed in the yard. Instead, we have a hunting party in the marshes where they can dig to their hearts' content.

Puppy Playschool

Dixie, the Dobermann, is the puppy from hell. At least that is what her owner thinks about her. As far as Dixie is concerned, her human is simply a very tall and abominably slow dog and, alas, often rather tiresome and fickle.

"I'm at the end of my rope." The effusive young woman sitting across the desk from me in my office is so distraught her voice is quavering.

"I thought I was doing everything right. I read several books on dog training. I took her through a puppy training class, but she was completely distracted by the other dogs, and when I put a choke chain on her she just lay down and wouldn't move. She learned nothing."

Sharon's words are bubbling out ceaselessly, and she is hyperventilating.

"She doesn't know what No! means and when I say Leave It!, she just ignores me or runs away. It's impossible to let her off the leash, because she's so hard to catch and I am afraid she'll get hit by a car. Yet when she's on leash, she pulls so strongly I can hardly hold her."

Surely, any moment now, Sharon is going to float away with a superabundance of oxygen. But she anchors herself by clutching the arms of her chair and goes on with relentless vehemence. "I have a job where I can take my dog to work, but now they've given me an ultimatum: Either she learns to behave or I can't bring her any longer. I think it's unfair to leave a little puppy alone at home, day after day, for ten hours or more, but if I can't make her behave I won't

53

be able to keep her. I fear she is incorrigible."

The young woman picks anxiously at a thread sticking out from the upholstery of the chair she occupies.

"If you don't stop that, you'll take my office apart, one thread at a time, before your dog has a chance," I quip.

"Pardon?"

My vain attempt at levity drops like a lead balloon.

"I'm afraid I won't be able to keep my puppy if she can't be well behaved," the young woman blubbers.

Emotional outbursts by complete strangers always make me ill at ease. So I say, "Yes, I heard you the first time," a bit more brusquely than necessary. But it is time to stop this eruption.

In my twenty-five years of training dogs professionally, I have trained and helped train well over three thousand dogs. Hundreds of times I have found myself in the position of being the final bastion of "fixing" the dog or having him abandoned. This always fills me with a sense of dread, and failure is not an option. Of course, sometimes it is advantageous to find the dog a better home, but all too commonly, dogs cast out because of undesired behavior bounce from home to home. During this process the predicament often worsens, resulting in an animal that is so gravely disturbed behaviorally that only an expert could alleviate the wreckage; and since experts generally don't choose such canine reprobates, often the pitiable creature's last stop is permanent confinement and segregation in a back yard, or even death. For a social animal born to run, I don't know which fate is worse.

Sharon's five-month-old black and brown Dobermann bitch named Dixie sports a pair of enormous uncropped ears. They stick out to the side of her head rather like corkscrews, giving her a faint resemblance to the Flying Nun. Awkward on her gangly legs, she is adorable. While her owner recites the litany of her complaints, Dixie bumbles through my office on a hunting-and-gathering excursion that simulates a scatterbrained seek-and-destroy mission. Her attention span approximates zero point two seconds. She has hardly picked up an object when she spies something even more enticing, like a kitten gamboling from one ball of yarn to the next. Toys, pens, boxes, writing pads and plastic bottles falling prey to her indomitable inquisitiveness are gnawed a bit and quickly forsaken. No child in a toy store could be more ecstatic. Dixie is so enraptured that she is talking to herself. She makes little groaning, barking and singing sounds while she throws a crumpled piece of paper into the air, with a shake of her head that makes her ears flap like signal flags in a stiff breeze. She is immersed in a world of her own, fighting bottle dragons and hunting paper rabbits.

Her owner's anxious and incessant efforts to quell this onslaught with repeated expostulations of Leave it! or No! are completely ignored. When Dixie climbs onto a chair and assails a roll of paper towels hanging from a wall, Sharon, plainly mortified, bounds up to whisk her away. As merrily heedless and clumsy as Dixie may be most of the time, she dodges her owner with a sudden dexterity. Sharon gives up; outmaneuvered by the little rapscallion, she sags onto a chair.

I have seen and heard quite enough. I rip off a paper towel and offer it to Dixie, who is unexpectedly reluctant to take it from my hand. When I wave it in the air and coax her to me, the puppy snatches it and in a flash recoils to a safe distance, out of the reach of my arm.

At my questioning glance to Sharon, she hazards an explanation. "She is not allowed to play with paper, because she steals Kleenexes and empties waste baskets at work and shreds everything. In puppy class she was supposed to learn

Barking Up the Right Tree

Leave it! I was taught to offer her something she wasn't allowed to have with one hand, like a piece of paper or some food, and when she reached for it we would say Leave it, and push her away. Then, when she looked away, we were told to feed her a treat with the other hand."

I want to tear my hair and shout, You ninny! The only thing you taught your puppy is to distrust you. If you want to play stupid games go to Las Vegas, for chrissakes!

But that would be uncultured. Moreover, it really isn't Sharon's fault when she is given idiotic advice. Inwardly, I tear my hair and shout. Outwardly, I take a deep breath and remark pointedly, "As you said, that approach was extraordinarily ineffectual."

I ask Sharon not to interfere while I play with Dixie. She (Sharon, not Dixie) still looks so tense that I am tempted to offer her a chew toy to calm her nerves, but instead I say something soothing. "If she destroys anything in my office I won't hold you responsible, okay?"

While Dixie continues her rampage, I pluck a piece of cardboard out of the wastebasket and, sitting on the floor, start playing with it, ignoring her completely. Dixie stops what she is doing and stares at my piece of cardboard with greedy eyes. When I tease her she latches on and starts to pull, but since I have no intention for the moment of surrendering my prized piece of cardboard, she cannot simultaneously grip onto it and stay out of my reach. She has two choices: to let go or endure my stroking her with my other hand. At first she fears reprisals and releases as soon as I touch her, but quickly she becomes bolder, and when she finally lets me stroke her, I release my grasp and relinquish the cardboard. Thrilled, she capers off with her booty, dancing past me at a safe distance. I make no attempt to recapture the conquered object. Instead, I briefly stroke her across her back every time she comes near. Emboldened by my apparent ineptitude, she thrusts her valuable possession at me, daring me to snatch it. I do, and this time she does not let go when I pat her. Once again, she is rewarded for not avoiding my hand by winning the toy.

"I was told never to play tug-o'-war or play roughly with her, so she wouldn't become dominant or aggressive," Sharon interrupts our game. "And I've also read that in several books on dog training," she adds to validate her position.

I would be permanently bald and hoarse if I gave in to my primal impulses. So, instead, I deliver a lengthy discourse on the state of dog training in general. First, however, we move our operation to my training field—before Dixie causes her owner apoplexy.

We leave Dixie safely to her hunting excavations for gophers and mice, while I ascend one of my soapboxes.

"The first dog-obedience training books I know of were written at the beginning of the twentieth century by men who were genuine dog lovers and had achieved superior powers of observation. Although some methods and assertions were questionable in the light of modern behavioral science, there was nothing indiscriminate or unsophisticated about their way of training. Since then, hundreds and quite possibly thousands of writers and dog trainers have regurgitated the same old punitive methods and dressed them up in a mantle of ego, in the process sacrificing all discernment in a one-method-fits-all approach. While these plagiarizers were (and, alas, still are) busy copying from each other, indisputable advances have been made in ethology, the scientific comparative behavioral research of animals. Reading just one serious book on ethology will give you infinitely more valuable information on dog training than all the training books (with a few notable exceptions) put together."

Barking Up the Right Tree

When my breath finally gives out, Sharon's eyes are glassy. (I sometimes have that effect on people, surely because they are dazzled rather than dazed.) While my peroration may not have convinced her, manifestly it has drained any resistance, rendering her promise to cooperate easily extracted.

"I am prepared to take a couple of weeks off work to train Dixie," Sharon offers. "They don't really want me back, anyway, with this little monster," she amplifies, with a lop-sided grin.

"Perfect!" I'm beginning to like this young woman; there is no mistaking the seriousness of her intent. And she does seem to have a good sense of humor, after all, an absolute necessity if she is to survive my kind of training. "In two weeks you'll be well on your way to being the great leader," I promise her.

Sharon appears relieved. "I'll do anything! I'll be consistent and firm—"

"You have done quite enough of that," I say. "Being consistent and firm is only the smallest part in educating a puppy. You will learn to put yourself in leadership position due to your superior ability, in a very similar way to what a dog mother would do. Don't think of dog training in terms of dominance and submission, but in terms of leader and follower. First, you are going to play with her the way another dog would. She will learn that you control all pleasant activities. *You* must be the gateway to doggie-paradise, not other dogs, not other people. You! She needs to understand that nothing gratifying happens without your playing a positive part in it. Right now she would rather amuse herself alone or with other dogs. She ignores you, because to her you are incomprehensible and a crashing bore," I admonish Sharon, not very graciously. "Do you ever play with your dog?"

Puppy Playschool

"Oh yes!" Sharon nods vigorously.

"Really? How?"

"Well ..." Now Sharon doesn't quite know how to respond. "I try to get her to fetch, but she's not particularly interested. I guess ... er ... no, I don't really play with her," she says, frowning and shaking her head slowly.

"Even if Dixie liked to play Fetch," I explain, "there are so many other games you can play. I pity the dog who only knows Fetch! Sharon, *all* dog games are in their nature either fighting or predatory games; there *is* nothing else. Not allowing Dixie to bite or tug and tear deprives her of practically all possibilities to play with you. No wonder she prefers the company of other dogs to yours."

"But I can learn to play with her, can't I? It's not too late?"

"Of course you can learn," I reassure her. "Please have a seat while I demonstrate the finer points of behaving like a dog."

I commence by crawling toward Dixie on all fours, patting my hands on the ground, bowing in front and sticking my rear in the air in a most unladylike fashion. If I had a tail I would wag it, but this will have to suffice. In my hand I am holding a knotted piece of burlap, waving it in front of Dixie's nose enticingly. Dixie is delighted and accepts my invitation to play by grabbing the rag and tugging vehemently. I roll onto my back and haul the burlap rag with the attached Dixie across my body where I take her in a headlock. She extricates herself, releases her grip on the toy and latches on to the arm of my sweatshirt instead, pinching a bit of skin in the process. Ouch! My free hand now assaults her from the rear and, undaunted, she releases my arm as she pirouettes to defend against this new peril. My other hand swoops down from above, jostling her to the ground. No matter how she struggles, this time I won't let her squirm out of the pin. After a few seconds she stops fidgeting and lies still for a moment. Immediately, I release and stroke her. While I speak to her gently and cheerfully, she munches at my unadorned ear, my earrings having long ago fallen victim to nibbling puppies. I wiggle the burlap rag and when she grips it, she is allowed to carry it away.

When I get up to fetch a couple of tennis balls Dixie follows me sanguinely. My remarkable savoir-faire of impersonating a superior dog has already begun to win her over. Sharon, by now already regretting that she has wasted good money on an outright lunatic, calls out, "She won't bring the ball back!"

"I know, you told me already. And why should she?" I retort, a trifle short-tempered. "Playing fetch may be your idea of fun; it clearly isn't hers."

When I throw the ball, Dixie, as anticipated, runs to pick it up, but then keeps going in a big arc. But I have planned ahead. Bouncing the second ball, I call Dixie, who immediately returns to me, tennis-ball number one in her mouth. Greed now puts her in a quandary: She wants both balls! As soon as she drops ball number one, I throw ball two, enticing her to return by teasing her with ball one. Since Dixie is a talented dog, she learns very quickly that dropping a ball near me results in further play.

Next, I produce a long buggy whip with a tennis ball fastened to the end. Now I can make the ball bounce, scurry and speed along the ground like a small prey animal. We call it Puppy Fishing. Dixie is instantly hooked. When she catches the ball, the springy action of the tip of the buggy whip provides enough resistance for her to fight without damaging her teeth, and when released, the tennis ball is catapulted into action. I have to call a stop to this game, because Dixie would play until she departed this world from exhaustion. When I rejoin Sharon, Dixie tumbles down to take a nap almost at once.

"Excellent! You've got a real dog, not a white mouse!" I announce.

Sharon evidently is considering the likelihood that white mice in my brain have gnawed through several vital connections. "What do you mean—white mouse?" she asks suspiciously.

"White mice are specially bred strains for use in laboratories," I explain. "They are much easier to handle than their gray counterparts, because they are essentially white lumps that don't do much more than breed, eat and—er—eliminate. Most of their species-specific motor patterns have been bred out of them. Quite a few dogs are just like that. Many people don't want to make the effort to deal with a creature that acts like a dog, so the market provides dogs with the abilities and personalities of door stops. It's a sorry development. Now we have working breeds that cannot do what they were originally bred to do. People who want dogs to behave like potted plants should get a rubber tree or at the most turtles or guinea pigs."

"There are times when I wish Dixie behaved like a potted plant," Sharon admits. "Then I could take her to work and it would make my life a lot easier."

"Oh Sharon, you would get bored out of your mind with such a dog. I think when she is trained you will be thrilled that you have a dog that you can *do* something with. "Dixie is very talented, indeed," I assure Sharon.

"You think she's trainable?" she asks hopefully, but there is skepticism in her voice. My discourse has evidently not convinced her.

"Piece of cake!" I wave a nonchalant hand. "But like all

talented, eager young dogs, she needs to exercise the skills nature has given her, and she needs to learn to trust you. No matter how gifted, no dog truly understands the vague and abstract concepts of No and Leave it. What do you really mean when you give those commands?"

"Well—" Sharon hasn't a clue what I am talking about and gives me a bewildered stare. "Get out of the garbage, don't jump, give back my sock, slow down, don't pull—"

"—don't bark, don't chase the ducks, stay here and don't approach that other dog, don't run out the door, don't roll in that disgusting stuff, don't eat that disgusting stuff, don't bug me, etc., etc., etc.," I proceed with the catalogue.

"She couldn't possibly understand all of that," Sharon says, a flicker of comprehension in her eyes. "But what do I say when I don't want her to do something? How do I say, No?" she asks anxiously.

"You don't say No or Leave it, you—" I try to elucidate.

"Besides, she sometimes does understand and stops doing naughty things," Sharon crows. "When I say No—"

The flicker, alas, has gone out again.

My exasperated intake of air and my not very surreptitious glance to the heavens stop her in mid-sentence. "She understands nothing!" I declare. "Nothing useful, that is. When she hears your angry voice she reacts by freezing—or at the very least by being emotionally stunned—the same way a puppy would duck or be petrified when an adult dog barks or growls at it. She understands she is in trouble and that the danger is coming from you. No wonder she does not come! It is sometimes okay to elicit a freeze response when there is real danger, such as when she is chewing on an electrical cord. But if the negative command is overused, the puppy only learns to ignore you or be afraid of you. You must tell her what she should do instead of what not to do."

Sharon ponders this for a moment. "It's not really Dixie; it's all about training me, isn't that true? You're saying that if I knew what I was doing I wouldn't have so many problems with her."

Ah, the propitious moment when the light dawns at last!

"Indeed! In the course of changing your behavior and learning to communicate with her effectively, you will teach your dog to respond to you positively and predictably. But make no mistake; changing your behavior is much harder than it sounds. You will be tempted to fall back into old patterns. When that happens, stop. Have a cup of tea (or something stronger) and think the matter through before you act."

Sharon smiles and nods eagerly, but long experience tells me that more elaboration is needed.

"To be consistent for the sake of consistency is wrong. It is only beneficial if a certain approach is successful. Repeating something ineffectual a thousand times will not miraculously improve results. *The right approach will show incipient success almost at once.* When the beginnings are made, we then set out to gradually perfect the exercise. Therefore, each time you interact with Dixie, observe and ask yourself if you are getting the desired result. If not, take the time to think it through and change your approach. Dogs communicate primarily with their bodies. Therefore, your most important tool of motivation is the appropriate body language. Dog training consists of so much more than giving treats or punishing at the proper times. How effectively you communicate with your dog is based on how well you understand inborn behavior and how competently you use body language. We will work on this during every lesson. For now, you will get five homework assignments, which you must follow assiduously. Agreed?"

Barking Up the Right Tree

Sharon nods so vigorously that I am afraid her head is going to snap off.

"First, and most important," I persist, "you will play with Dixie every day at least twice until she is exhausted; more is better. Get on the floor and wrestle with her, and don't worry if she bites you a little in her enthusiasm. However, she needs to recognize all the time that you are stronger, faster and smarter. In a wrestling game you *always* win! However, in a tug-o'-war game you should let *her* win the booty. Play with two balls and with the Puppy Fishing toy.

"Second, at home, after you have worn her out, you put her on a short tie-down, about a foot and a half long, just enough so she can comfortably lie down but not get entangled. You can move the tie-down so that she is in your company all the time, but not the center of attention. If she fusses, simply ignore her. Start with fifteen-minute increments and work gradually up to two hours. Do not take her off tie-down while she gripes. In two weeks you can take the tie-down to work.

"Third, if she steals an unapproved toy, such as your shoe, don't get hysterical. Take another toy and tease her with it. You tease Dixie not by holding the toy out like a stick of candy toward her, but by pretending that *you* are interested in this new toy. She will become envious of your possession and you can trade easily. She will be tricked, and by the time she finds out that she has made a bad bargain, you have hidden the shoe. You can also trade for a treat. For the time being, do not take anything out of her mouth, unless it is an emergency.

"Fourth, when she comes to you, she must be rewarded with small treats and a little enthusiastic outburst of joy on your part every single time, without fail. Oh, I almost forgot: Let her have the confounded [I may have used a slightly more forceful term] Kleenexes or cardboard pieces—they won't harm her. Better yet, give her the cardboard of paper-towel rolls or boxes (with staples and plastic tape removed) to rip up and eat if she wants.

"Fifth, throw Dixie's strangulation chain away and, whenever possible, walk Dixie on a Flexi-Line, on a normal buckle collar, to give her more freedom and to prevent her *and you* from building up a pulling habit."

In the course of the following week I hear nothing from Sharon. My customary sanguine nature—along with twenty-five years of experience—tells me that no news is good news, so I resist the impulse to call and see how the training is progressing. But some apprehension always plagues me when I am uncertain about the owner's ability to assimilate my coaching. Thus I await Sharon's next lesson somewhat anxiously.

There is Dixie at a quasi gallop—oh no!—dragging Sharon across the parking lot to the training field, Sharon's free hand flailing to keep her balance. My heart sinks to my grass-stained sneakers and I brace myself for the list of complaints sure to follow.

"I haven't had time to exercise her today." Sharon smiles, somewhat short of breath, as she unleashes Dixie, figuratively and literally. "I thought she could burn some energy here."

The young Dobermann shoots off and Sharon reaches for the Puppy Fishing toy. In a flash Dixie is back, jumping in the air, urging her owner to start playing.

"This is her favorite toy," Sharon reports happily. "She knows exactly where I keep it. Yesterday, I was called into work unexpectedly. I took her with me and—"

My eyes widen in dismay. "Sharon, that's too soon, she is not ready to—"

Barking Up the Right Tree

"— and she did beautifully," Sharon continues, unperturbed. "I took her out first to play with her, and at work she was on tie-down. They only needed me for a few hours, anyway, and Dixie slept the whole time. At home my life is a lot easier. I don't sweat the little stuff anymore, and I've put everything out of her reach and a lid on the garbage. She comes, well, most of the time, but she doesn't run away anymore when I come to get her. I think she likes me better than before. If she never learned anything else, I could live with her now."

Sharon has taken the first and biggest hurdle, inducing Dixie to accept and, indeed, desire her benevolent leadership.

"Now that you have won — not tried to force — Dixie's attention, we can really start to train her. Now it will be easy," I promise. "Let's start the first phase of teaching her to come reliably and quickly when called. I call it the Rocket Recall."

I hold Dixie by the collar and ask Sharon to run away in a straight line. When she turns and calls her dog, I release Dixie who now streaks toward Sharon, ears fluttering, as fast as her gangly legs can carry her. As soon as she arrives, Sharon feeds her numerous little treats, one at a time, to maximize the benefit and to induce Dixie to pay attention to her for an extended period of time.

"Wow! She has never come this fast," Sharon exclaims, beaming. "What makes it work so well?"

"Good question," I commend her. "Actually, there are three reasons. One, seeing you *run* away rather than just walk makes her want to chase you. Two, the great distance between her and you makes her afraid she might lose you, particularly since you left with a bag of treats in your pocket, which, in Dixie's mind, increases your net worth. Three, my holding her by the collar frustrates her, since she cannot act on her impulses. Frustration builds intensity."

Sharon nods earnestly. "That makes sense."

"You should repeat this exercise at least one hundred times over the next week." Now I am fully confident that she will follow any reasonable instruction to the letter. "Make a game out of it. Do you have someone to assist you?"

Sharon intends to recruit her boyfriend for the task and to press some of her more agreeable colleagues into service.

When she returns the following week for her lesson, Sharon reports proudly that Dixie is not only welcome at her place of work, but also that a few of her colleagues help her with her Rocket Recall during the lunch hour.

"They love it!" Sharon gushes. "They stand in line so they can hold Dixie and see her run. Everyone wants to play Puppy Fishing with her. For the rest of the afternoon she is so worn out, I don't even have to have her on tie-down any-more. In fact, I pretty much only use it when I am in a meet-ing. I take her out to play and run before I go to work, and if she gets restless, ten minutes of Puppy Fishing will just about put her into a state of suspended animation for a couple of hours."

Needless to say I am overjoyed at Sharon and Dixie's progress. The first big hurdle—bonding—is taken, and there is no more talk of having to give Dixie up. Sharon and Dixie are ready for the next step in training.

I usually don't spend a lot of time on Sit, because most dogs have a rudimentary understanding of it by the time they are enrolled in my lessons. It is not only the easiest exercise, but also the minor skill many owners drill to the point of revulsion. It compares to sloppily playing "Merrily We Roll Along" five hundred times on the piano and considering that a stepping-stone to performing Beethoven. It is commonly taught by holding a treat over the dog's nose and rewarding when the dog sits, or by the cruder method of pushing on the dog's rear. In terms of control over the dog it is almost useless. Dixie's next exercise, therefore, is the first phase of the Down.

Now, when I say Down, I am in no way referring to the slow, casual lying down that so many owners confuse with an effective command. Usually, the dog plops himself on his behind first, in something akin to a sitting position, and cogitates on whether or how he should proceed from there. He then walks his front feet forward (generally after repeated pleas from his owner, who is inanely pointing to the ground as if the dog had the option to fly away instead) and leisurely sinks into a lying position. The owner now augments his command with the completely superfluous Stay, even though it is clearly not possible, for man or dog, to lie down and walk away at the same time.

The Down I have in mind is altogether different. In its finished version, the dog drops to the ground in one fluid, rapid motion, even from a gallop, and remains motionless until he hears the release command. He complies instantly, even at a distance. Taught in this way, the Down becomes a safety switch; the dog can be shut down instantly if he is in danger or about to engage in some unpopular activity. Together with a speedy and unequivocal recall, the owner has absolute voice control over his dog. All other formal exercises are ornamental.

Sharon begins by showing Dixie a handful of treats and when Dixie displays interest, lowers her closed fist to the ground, without giving any command. Dixie now experiments with several behaviors to see which one will yield the food. She pokes and probes with her nose; she sits and peers expectantly in Sharon's eyes; she barks and scratches with her foot; she licks Sharon's face. At length, in exasperation, she lies down, elbows first, to stay as close to the food as possible. As soon as Dixie's elbows and rear touch the ground, Sharon opens her fist and *places the delicious morsels between Dixie's forelegs.* As long as her puppy stays down, Sharon steadily trickles tidbits between Dixie's legs. When the young Dobermann gets up, feeding stops. No commands or reproaches of any kind are given. The exercise is simply repeated in a slightly different location.

If the dog is hungry, the learning curve is remarkably steep. After only three or four repetitions, spirited Dixie hits the deck every time Sharon's fist is on the ground. Only now is Sharon permitted to say Down.

"Tell me again why I'm not supposed to feed from my hand," Sharon asks. Like most students, Sharon finds it difficult to focus on her dog and listen at the same time.

"If you do not put the food on the ground, the dog will orient to your hand and follow it instead of staying down. Your hand then works like a lure and that is counterproductive, unless you want to point to the ground forever."

"Yeah, that makes sense," Sharon acknowledges. "And why am I not supposed to say Down before she lies down?"

"Because Dixie doesn't know Down yet, and she can't look up the meaning of the word in a dictionary. She needs to associate the word with the correct position. Dogs don't think; they can only associate. Of course, once she *comprehends* the Down, then you can give the command and Dixie will comply."

The remainder of the session Dixie is allowed to romp with selected dogs, both young and old, to further her canine social skills. I am no advocate of chance socialization at the dog park, but instead make sure that my young charge is learning exactly the lessons I want her to learn from her fellow dogs, namely confidence without being a bully.

At her next lesson, Sharon enters with Dixie and not the other way around. The young Dobermann impatiently waits for the obedience practice to commence. Obedience has become a game to her. The rules are understood, but at this time not strictly enforced. As expected, Dixie throws herself on the ground as soon as she anticipates the Down exercise.

"Is this okay?" Sharon asks.

"You have done a wonderful job, Sharon." The approbation is sincere. "I wish everyone would learn as fast," I add, somewhat wistfully.

"No, I mean, is it okay that she jumps the gun on the exercise?"

"Absolutely. Anticipation is a step toward learning. For the time being don't correct her. I would like you to proceed with continuous positive motivation for a few more weeks. Then you switch gradually to intermittent rewards. She is only six months old and very immature; that's too young to pressure her into absolute compliance. By the time she is around a year of age, we will teach her that obedience, although pleasant, is not entirely optional. Congratulations! You and Dixie have graduated from Puppy Playschool!"

Life With
the Schnauzer Family
The World Is a Safe Place

Two or three times a week I take the Schnauzerkinder along to Ilka's, Schnupp's and Grendel's Schutzhund or Search and Rescue training. The veteran German Shepherd Dogs, Ben and Gandhi, have already been retired and Falko had a forced retirement due to a back injury.

Schutzhund is an international versatility dog sport, in which the dog's disposition is evaluated for strength of drives, emotional and physical resilience, willingness to work and appropriate reaction to danger. It consists of tracking, obedience and agility, and a simulated protection phase. There are three progressively more difficult levels. The lower levels also serve as basic training for police dogs. While the adult dogs have to be well-behaved and controlled and wait their turn in their crates, puppies are given a lot of leeway. They greet the other trainers and clamber on the bleachers, accosting and jumping at everybody for treats and pats. The bite-helper, who plays his part as the bad guy convincingly during the protection phase, is their special friend. His protective leather gear makes him nearly invulnerable, at least to young dogs, and the Schnauzerkinder are allowed to bite and tumble and wrestle with him.

I lay particular emphasis on socializing my young dogs with people, adults and children alike, who are completely unafraid and uninhibited with them without trying to push them around, emotionally or physically. It's amazing to me how many complete strangers seem to feel the compulsion to give somebody else's dog commands and instructions.

Likewise, I socialize the Schnauzerkinder with other dogs, both puppies and adults, who neither bully nor defer to them. Training situations where I can meet with like-minded dog owners are, of course, ideal for this purpose. There will be time enough to meet the fearful little old lady and the impulsive child, as well as the socially ill-adjusted dog, when the Schnauzerkinder are older.

At home I do not usually inflict my dogs on unsuspecting guests. They are put in a run for that time. (The dogs, not the guests, although sometimes I would find the opposite vastly more entertaining.) Should particularly doughty souls express the desire to meet any of my dogs, they are forewarned. Quite naturally, new people in the house are an irresistible focus of activity. I really don't understand what could be gained by ruining half the evening by trying to keep a young or vivacious dog out of some visitor's hair or the chicken-salad bowl. The guest usually detests being accosted by his host's dog; the dog is constantly and ineffectively reprimanded; and the owner feels like an idiot.

When I was younger and more imprudent, those guests who proclaimed they liked animals were often put through a trial by fire meeting my young dogs.

"They are just a little exuberant. They'll calm down in a little while," I'd say, blithely ignoring the pained or terrified expressions on my friends' faces.

The notion of becoming a wild-eyed old lady, living alone with fifty dogs in a house on the hill, barking to myself while preparing doggie chow and warding off intruders by brandishing a pooper-scooper, flashed in my mind. I have since

The World Is a Safe Place

come to the insight that Love-me, love-my-dog is a silly position to take.

Like a Bolt
of Lightning

If the task at hand were only to get our dogs to perform certain behaviors in return for food, toys or a friendly pat on the back, few of us would have difficulty training them. In practice, however, and often when it is least convenient, the dog is more strongly motivated by distractions, like other dogs or a running rabbit, than by proffered treats.

Dixie is now a year old. Sharon reports that the young Dobermann, although obedient most of the time, is often rather dilatory in complying if there is something more amusing to pursue than treats or a little game, such as digging for mice or eating or rolling in some unspeakable substance. A few months ago Sharon would have considered even this degree of obedience ideal, but now she has learned that she can expect more from her dog.

Dixie has indeed become a teenager. Her formerly huge ears now fit the size of her head and her awkward filly gait has become a ground-covering elastic stride. The world has opened up to her and she has the mind and the confidence to explore and experience it all. When Sharon puts her in a Down position with treats, Dixie eats the food, but it is evident that at least half her mind is on the wonderful birds she is going to chase as soon as she gets up.

"You are right," I say to Sharon, "it's time to teach her a new lesson. So far she has learned that obeying results in rewards; obedience is good. However, she hasn't learned that *not* obeying is bad, because it results in a mildly disagreeable consequence. In other words, now she must learn that obeying is not only good, but also the only safe choice she has."

"So now we jerk her around on a choke collar?" inquires Sharon with a grimace. I forgive her question, because I remember that she has read too many worthless books on dog training.

"We'll do nothing of the sort," I appease her. "You've done your homework; Dixie is well-bonded and well-prepared. She only needs a little physical and emotional pressure for emphasis. We'll use a normal collar, no choking necessary. The idea is to startle Dixie with a snap of the leash and a loud voice when she makes an *obviously preventable* mistake, because of her *inattention*. She will quickly learn that in order to avoid being startled, her safest choice is to comply with a command she understands very well."

"I'm a little concerned about this leash-snapping business," Sharon objects. "At the dog park I've heard some dog owners claim that you can train a dog by purely positive motivation."

"Ah, the dog-park experts! The armchair specialists! The master trainers who managed to get one dog, or perhaps even two, through a basic obedience class! Those dog owners?" I ask sarcastically, softening my comment with a sweet, if not completely genuine, smile.

"Yeah, well, it is true, their dogs are not that well-controlled," Sharon acknowledges, a bit reluctantly. "Not according to *your* standards," she adds, giving me a quick grin.

"Using positive motivation exclusively works very well in a controlled environment where all, or at least most, variables are predictable," I explain.

"Like dolphins or sea otters in an aquarium." She's catching on.

"Exactly. It does not produce reliable obedience under unpredictable circumstances, although I agree that you can accomplish a lot more with positive motivation alone than was recognized a few decades ago."

"And it doesn't work reliably because—" Sharon hesitates.

"If Dixie is walked off leash (as she should be), she is bound to encounter more enticing motivation, sooner or later," I complete her sentence.

"Like a cat or a rabbit jumping up in front of her," Sharon follows my train of thought. "But," she looks thoughtful, "I've heard some people boast they can call their dog away from a running deer, without having used force during their training. Do you think they were lying—er—exaggerating?"

"Not necessarily," I concede. "But I strongly suspect that those dogs were not highly motivated to chase deer in the first place. They might not have had high prey drive; perhaps they were overweight or very timid or simply phlegmatic dogs by nature. It is no masterpiece to control a lump."

"A white mouse," Sharon grins.

"Yes, exactly. The quick, willful, enthusiastic dog, however, is not effectively controlled by positive motivation alone."

"Like Dixie," Sharon nods at the young Dobermann.

"Yes, like Dixie," I agree. "Besides, it is absurd, or at the very least uninformed, to believe that in nature canines learn without ever experiencing external pressure. The young dog's elders *do* pressure him into compliance."

"I never thought of that," Sharon says pensively, "but of course you are right."

As so often, I cannot resist the urge to commence an enlightening discourse: Positive Motivation or Training With Positive Reinforcement have become a buzzwords in the dog-training world. More due to ideological reasons than to profound knowledge of canine behavior, many dog trainers have let themselves become polarized into two extreme positions: In the one camp are the trainers who abhor pressuring the dog in any way. In the other camp we find those trainers who want no part of positive motivation with food and toys. But most effective dog-training schools of thought are (and always have been) found on a *continuum* between purely positive motivation and forcing the dog to comply. Even the dog trainers around the turn of the last century maintained that the goal must be to motivate the dog to work joyfully. Today, none of the trainers on the cutting edge can be located at either extreme. (Frankly, I believe only the simple-minded and those who profit from them can be found there.) Gradually, over the course of several decades, the balance has shifted toward training more with positive motivation, which is a good development.

"Look, Sharon, we are not just going to jerk poor little Dixie around. She has to learn that a snap at the collar simply means to pay attention. We teach her that the snap is a positive signal, not something to be feared. The problem is not pressure per se, but *inappropriate* pressure. A little stress makes the dog react and learn fast. But as the stress level goes up beyond a certain threshold or if it stays up, the ability to constructively process information goes down. This is true for dogs and people. If I suddenly started shoving you and yelling, you would view my action as an attack and you would react either with alarm or confusion, or you'd fight back. In any case, you wouldn't stay calm and ponder what I possibly could have meant by my bizarre action."

"I think I'd be flustered, and then I'd shove back," Sharon agrees. "And you'd deserve it," she nods with a smirk.

"So I would. But I won't shove you and we won't jerk

silly little Dixie around. We'll use our brains to train Dixie, not our brawn. I'll demonstrate."

I begin by walking briskly, holding Dixie on a loose leash. When she least expects it and without prior warning, I snap the leash lightly. Instantly, before she has the chance to feel sorry for herself, I throw a ball in the air and let her play with it. The next time, right at the moment when she feels startled, but before she becomes anxious, I throw a piece of food in the air and let her catch it, praising her profusely. Incrementally, I snap the collar harder while always keeping some intensity in reserve. In other words, I never snap the leash as strongly as I plan on doing during the exercise in which I'll compel the obedience.

Very quickly Dixie understands that a yank at the collar precedes a pleasant activity and she snaps to attention each time she feels her collar twitch. It is remarkable how fast dogs learn when they think that they can benefit.

Sharon is to practice this exercise, compulsion as positive signal, with Dixie for the next week. She also must intensify her rewards for the Recall, Sit and Down exercises.

The use of compulsion in training is always a double-edged sword. I venture to say that all those dog trainers who can now pressure a dog effectively and with finesse made their share of errors early on. Therefore, I don't trust beginning dog trainers to have the correct timing and whenever possible, I introduce the dog to systematic compulsion myself. Dixie is on a leash and I tell her to lie down. To make it easy I put treats on the ground, just as we did in the beginning. No sooner has Dixie finished her treats when she becomes restless and bored, but I observe her closely and am prepared for what I know must come next: Dixie commences to stand up. As soon as her feet move, *before* she is all the way up, I thunder, "Down!" and snap the leash. My body language and my voice convey very clearly that this is no joke. Since I have no intention of really hurting Dixie, I make sure that my bluff is believable. Dixie gives a little startled yelp and falls back instantly on the behavior that has been conditioned for many months: She throws herself on the ground and lies motionless, eyes wide. My body language changes immediately. I assume a relaxed, non-confrontational body posture as I stroke her over her back, speaking to her soothingly. After I release her, I play with her boisterously to ameliorate the after-effects of startling her. Under no circumstances do I pressure Dixie so strongly that she cannot be easily reassured or that she becomes frightened of me.

Once Dixie has learned that it is not *her* decision to end the exercise by getting up, but mine to release her from a Down, the next step—namely, teaching her that it is also my decision to *begin* the exercise—is easy and requires no further pressure on the dog. After only a couple of repetitions, Dixie hurls herself to the ground and remains motionless. I insist on rapid compliance, giving her no time to become worried or confused. She already *knows* that Down is a good and safe position.

Now it is Sharon's turn. She takes Dixie and starts walking with her. As she gets ready to enforce the Down, Sharon slows to a funereal pace and fumbles with the leash. Portentously turning toward Dixie, she asks softly, "Down?" The inflection of her voice is more suited to the question, Could you spare the time to lie down, pleeease?

Dixie subsides slowly, confusion on her face. Sharon reacts by jiggling the leash indecisively and repeating her request. Now the dog is cowering, her ears flat against her head, staring up at her owner with undisguised consternation.

Like a Bolt of Lightning

"Stop!" I bellow. "Stop that!" Waving my hands wildly like a demented window cleaner, I charge toward Sharon.

"What the hell are you doing?" I say sharply, raising my hands to the heavens. "Either give your dog a command or invite her to tea—don't do both at the same time! Weren't you watching?"

In long years of experience I have learned that it is a tactical error to sweet-talk an owner who is cosseting her dog inappropriately, that is to say, at the wrong time. Many novice dog trainers need a burst of adrenaline to overcome their doubts in their own abilities to be effectively forceful with their dogs. More experienced trainers are able to mimic the necessary threat to the dog without a great investment of emotion.

Sharon has learned some time ago that my bark is worse than my bite, but she grimaces. "Show me again."

Dixie is still a little daunted by Sharon's clumsy attempt. Therefore, I run with her, leaping in the air at times or breaking into a skip. Dixie is delighted and bounds by my side. Abruptly, without giving her any warning, either in my demeanor or by fumbling with the leash, I swing around toward her with the speed of lightning and thunder, "Down!"

Dixie reacts at once; there is no need to yank the leash.

"You didn't see her cowering with *me*, did you?" I resume with my customary disarming directness as I hand Sharon the leash. "Your command and your movements have to be quick and sharp as lightning. And it all needs to come out of the clear blue sky. The point is for Dixie to be *startled*, so she has no time to become worried and mount resistance. Don't signal your intent with your body beforehand."

This time Sharon gets it right. I am not sure who is more startled, Dixie at her owner's unexpected vim or Sharon at her newfound mettle.

Sharon takes Dixie home with the promise to practice her Down under progressively more distracting circumstances.

"Don't forget," I remind her, "quick as lightning! *And only practice two or at most three Downs per session!* When you teach the exercise with positive motivation, many repetitions are needed. When you use compulsion, a little goes a long way."

Returning the following week, Sharon proudly shows off her training accomplishments. Dixie flings herself to the ground even from a run and remains there until Sharon releases her.

"It was easy," Sharon beams, "it really took only a few corrections. In the beginning she was a bit cowed, but that went away the third day or so. I haven't had to yank the leash or raise my voice in days now. When she did it well, I always praised and stroked her and sometimes rewarded her with food. I remembered you said intermittent reward strengthens the behavior, constant reward weakens it," she recounts proudly like a well-taught pupil. "Oh, I almost forgot: When I worked her in the park, a few times there were dogs whose owners made no effort to call them back, even though these people must have seen that I was working with Dixie. I tried to keep her down, but when the other dogs jumped at her, I guess she had no choice but to get up. Should I have made her remain down, anyway?"

"No, Sharon, you used excellent judgment. As trainers we always have to discern whether the dog is *unable* or *unwilling* to comply in order to act appropriately. Under the circumstances, Dixie had no choice but to get up; otherwise she would have made herself vulnerable, and no sane dog is going to do that. It really annoys me how many dogs are barely under voice control. Their owners blithely seem to think it is good enough that their dogs are friendly and don't run away. I just cannot understand—"

Before I can take root on my soapbox, Sharon brings me back to the issue at hand. "I really wanted her to lie down at a distance sometimes, but I must be doing something wrong. She always came to me first."

"Of course she would come to you. All the Downs she has done up to this point were near you. In order to train for the Drop at a Distance we need to have accomplished two preliminary exercises: One, she must drop and stay in the Down position even under distraction, and two, the recall has to be instantaneous and reliable, even under the strongest distraction."

"And the recall is what we have to enforce now," Sharon observes correctly. "But how? I can't imagine. But I'll bet you have a trick up your sleeve!"

"Indeed," I say, false modesty not being one of my failings. "We are going to recruit the help of the Holy Ghost, or better yet, of Thor in the Heavens!" I raise my voice and an index finger for emphasis.

Sharon says nothing, but her face seems to declare, Just when I was beginning to think Vera is peculiar, but at least she doesn't seem to be dangerous.

But I continue undaunted. "Thor will hurl a flash of lightning at Dixie's posterior when she ignores your calling her. At least that is what Dixie will be thinking. She will be seeking security with you when that happens. She already knows that coming is good. Now she'll learn it is her safest choice."

"But how—" Sharon begins.

"We'll use a Throw Chain," I say, producing a chain collar with a little bell attached to it.

"And we'll throw it at Dixie when she isn't listening," Sharon concludes.

"It's not quite as simple as that. Since the chain is supposed to *startle* Dixie, it is imperative that she not see you throw it. The more her focus is away from you and the less she expects it, the more she will be caught unawares and the more effective this technique will be. Furthermore, if she sees you throw it at her, she'll be afraid of you and not come to you. For all Dixie knows, this chain could have come out of the blue sky, like Thor's lightning. When you call her she'll come to you to be comforted. Very quickly she will realize that you have an ally in the sky and that coming immediately when you call her is the only safe course of action if she does not wish to incur Thor's wrath."

"She almost never listens when she is digging for mice, and she always sticks her rear in the air, so it would be easy to hit. But perhaps she can't hear me because her head is in a hole. No, I guess not." She grins when she sees me shaking my head.

"But I still have one more question," she continues. "Dixie sometimes bolts away to greet another dog or chase a bird; I'm afraid I won't be fast enough and she'll be out of range before I get my act together."

I am always gratified when my students begin to think like dog trainers. Sharon is taking her first steps, weighing the consequences of her actions in regards to Dixie. And what's more, she is becoming aware of the importance of anticipating Dixie's behavior. Timing and appropriate body language are vital elements in dog training. If the trainer's timing is even a little bit faulty, the whole effort could be wasted, or worse, be harmful to the dog and wreck the training process. If timing is off during the positive-motivation phase, no great damage is done, although the exercise may not be successful. Wrong timing during the compulsion phase, however, does great harm.

Like a Bolt of Lightning

"Let me give you an example. Let's say you have just roasted a chicken. The smell is wonderful and Dixie is very intrigued by the goings-on in the kitchen. Indeed, you've stumbled over her a couple of times and chased her out of the room. You place the chicken on top of the counter, to let it sit for a while before carving it. Meanwhile, you busy yourself again at the stove making gravy."

"I'm getting hungry," laughs Sharon.

"So is Dixie. Or rather, she's been hungry all along, hoping for an opportunity to procure some nourishment for a starving Dobermann."

"Yeah! She's always ready to consume food. If I left it up to her, I think she'd eat until she exploded."

"Most dogs are like that, and their well-meaning but uninformed owners let them become morbidly obese. But that is another soapbox," I digress. "Let me get on with my little scenario. While you are peering intently into the refrigerator to find the cream, you hear a thunderous crash and when you wheel around you see Dixie streaking out through the dog door with the chicken in her jaws."

"That is a very possible scenario," Sharon nods.

"The big question is, *when* do you correct her? Think before you answer."

"Well, I already know that correction after the fact is not only not successful, but actually harms the dog. What I was always taught is that you need to catch the dog in the act." Sharon smiles at me proudly, clearly expecting to be commended for having repeated this often-heard axiom.

"*Wrong!*" I shake my head. "This Catch Him in the Act business must have been invented by someone who was incapable of understanding his dog. He certainly had only a muddled idea of how animals learn."

"But—but that's what all the dog-training books I read

85

said," Sharon demurs.

"Oh Sharon, don't get me started. If these people studied animal behavior instead of copying from each other, the same rubbish wouldn't be repeated into eternity."

It is well-documented that behavior is most successfully modified *right before* the action takes place. Once the action is in progress it is difficult if not impossible to interrupt it, let alone re-direct it. Once the dog achieves success, the learning connection has been formed. Punishing after *or during* a particular action is merely a venting of anger on the trainer's part, and it is fruitless. In our case of the purloined chicken, the trainer must observe her dog carefully and anticipate when Dixie is about to steal the chicken. *Then* the trainer intercepts by shouting at the dog and descending on her like an avenging angel. Simply speaking, the trainer must correct the thought, not the action. Fortunately for us, dogs are poor poker players. They signal with their bodies what goes on in their minds. Just as we could not drive cars safely without anticipating constantly what other drivers are about to do, it is impossible to keep a dog off-leash without being aware of what she is going to do. With practice, this becomes very easy and almost second nature.

"So—" Sharon sums up after a brief hesitation, and I can see the gears moving in her head, "Thor has to hit Dixie with a flash of lightning just before she is about to bolt after another dog. Right?"

"Instant perfect dog!" Sharon bubbles at our next meeting. "I still can hardly believe how incredibly effective Thor's Chain is. I only had to throw it a few times, and she comes racing every time. Why didn't you tell me about this miracle cure a long time ago?"

"Because it isn't a miracle cure. It only worked with

Dixie, because you spent months preparing her for this moment. You have given her hundreds of positive experiences and, above all, no negative experiences when she comes. She trusts you unconditionally, because you have learned how she thinks and feels and you have learned to communicate with her in her own language. It stands to reason that dogs, not having spoken language, communicate with their bodies. You have learned to use this to your and Dixie's advantage."

"Well, anyway, it worked great," Sharon sums up.

"Sharon, had you not prepared Dixie, she would simply have run away or at least avoided you when she was startled by Thor's Chain. She would have had no earthly reason to come to you for protection. It worked because her bond to you is strong."

"Er—yes. The Drop at a Distance?" Sharon reminds me.

"Okay, you are ready for that now. As you have observed, when Dixie is at a distance and you say Down, she comes to you and lies down at your feet, simply because that's the way she learned it. What we have to teach her now is to stay in place; she already knows the Down."

"Do you have another miracle technique that works as well as Thor's Chain?" Sharon inquires hopefully.

"Of course! Although there really are no miracles in dog training. Muddled messages teach the dog the wrong things and clear messages beget desired, clear results. In other words—"

"Garbage in, garbage out!" Sharon interjects.

"Precisely! Anyway, as far as the Drop at a Distance is concerned, the secret, as always, lies in the right preparation, and there are no shortcuts for that. Here's how you do it: When Dixie is a distance away from you, you shout Down! and at the same time charge toward her with a forbidding demeanor, before she has a chance to come to you. This will give her the message, by way of your body language, that approaching you is not a good idea. The first couple of times you may need to *collide* with her. When she lies down before the collision occurs, you change your body language and walk calmly to her; stroke her, praise or reward her and release her. She will learn very quickly simply to lie down, instead of coming to you first. Let's try it."

As expected, Dixie picks up on the idea very rapidly. I send Sharon home to practice under various distractions.

"I've got a great story to tell you," Sharon says when she comes back with Dixie. "As you said, it only took a couple of days for Dixie to be quite reliable on her Down at a Distance. One time she got up early to run after another dog, but I jingled the chain immediately, before she took off, and when Dixie could hear Thor's chariot, the sound alone just about made her spin around, almost before I could call her. I didn't punish her, but simply told her to lie down again, and that time she didn't break her Down."

"That's why the recall needed to be solid, before we started on the Drop at a Distance," I nod. "Well, let's—"

"No, wait! You haven't heard my story yet," Sharon interrupts. "I was walking Dixie off the leash in a residential neighborhood and an animal-control van pulled up at the other side of the road. I thought the officer probably wanted to give me a ticket or a warning, so I played it cool. When I told Dixie to lie down, she dropped instantly on the spot and I sauntered over to the officer's window. He asked me if Dixie was my dog, as if that wasn't obvious, and when I agreed he said, 'I was going to give you a ticket, but seeing how well your dog is controlled, I won't. I wish everyone had their dog under control the way you do; it would make my job a lot easier. Have a nice day!' And then he drove off. I gave Dixie a big hug!"

Needless to say, I am elated by Sharon's success story.

"You know," Sharon is thinking aloud, "everyone likes Dixie at work; I'm really proud of her, and I love her in a way now that I didn't think possible before. I can take her anywhere and I can rely on her to respond to me instantly. And yet, she's not my little robot; she's got plenty of personality. It's like we are a team. Now that I'm having so much fun with her," she looks down, "I hardly can believe that I almost got rid of her."

Life With
the Schnauzer Family
The Babysitters

My friend Pat has come over to my house with her three-year-old daughter Amy who, much to her mother's astonishment, is a fastidious little girl with a penchant for toddler haute couture. She likes to wear ruffled dresses and patent-leather shoes and the like. Today she is clad in corduroy overalls and a frilly shirt. Her pride and joy is an enormous pink bow in her long blond hair. Perched on top of her head, it has a deplorable resemblance to a propeller.

"I'm sure she didn't get that sense of fashion from me," Pat groans.

Although Pat has a medium-sized dog at home and although my dogs are tolerant of children—if a bit boisterous at times—I have put them outside in their run. From previous visits I know that Amy has taken a special liking to Falko and Ilka.

Amy is bored with her coloring book and adult conversation and utters something in the gibberish that passes for language in toddlers.

"She wants to go outside and play with Falko and Ilka," Pat translates.

Generally, I don't think it is a good idea to leave any dog alone with a child below the age of reason, which I think most children reach at the age of twelve. However, I know Pat is a levelheaded woman, Amy a very nice child, and my

91

dogs tolerant but fully able to take care of themselves. Like all self-confident dogs, they would use their bodies and perhaps their voices to get their point across, and only if that failed would they be tempted to bite in earnest. In addition, they are very well-socialized with children of all ages.

It had been raining the previous day and the yard is rather muddy, but the deck is reasonably dry. Amy, Falko and Ilka busy themselves for a while, but soon Amy returns, blubbering at the top of her lungs.

At my concerned inquiry Pat shrugs, "Oh, Falko pushed her over."

Now, whereas Ilka, in spite of her vivacious and fiery disposition, is exceedingly gentle with children, Falko has a peculiar way of dealing with running toddlers: He snatches them by the seat of their pants or diapers, as the case may be. Thus abruptly deprived of locomotion, the child's torso topples forward, and when Falko releases, the toddler drops headlong. Falko has never so much as scratched a child and his is a very effective, albeit not always popular, way of controlling boisterous youngsters.

So Falko and Ilka remain outside and Amy is condemned to her coloring book. This doesn't last long, as could be expected. Amy desires to go out and play with the two dogs again. Pat now takes the only reasonable course of action.

"You can go out and play with Falko and Ilka," she tells her daughter, "but if you come in crying again, you stay inside and the dogs stay outside."

Amy nods; clearly she is aware that her mother means what she says.

We don't hear a peep from the trio for the next hour. It is beginning to get dark and Pat thinks it time to retrieve her daughter, who has disappeared from the deck. When she calls her, Falko comes up the stairs to the deck, Amy holding on to his ruff with her little fist to keep up with him and Ilka brings up the rear. Amy's cheeks are red like two polished apples, her blue eyes blazing and she is covered from head to toe with dirt, cheerfully unaware that her precious pink bow is probably lost forever in the muddy depths of my yard.

Puppy Plight
and Tyke Trouble

With the right guidance, dogs and children can be fabulous pals. Much depends on the parents' effective leadership in regards to both puppy and child.

My favorite kind of client, as one might imagine, is an owner who has a bit of intuitive or acquired understanding of animals and a generous helping of compassion, common sense and reason, along with a disposition that does not readily give way to nervous outbursts.

Judy is not one of these. She has brought me her four-month-old Golden Retriever puppy named Midas, a wary, almost furtive creature. For obscure reasons she found it necessary to inflict on me her chubby eight-year-old boy Alan, who is not furtive at all. This dreadful child treats my office as his personal toy store, with nary a sound of disapproval from his mother, who is at present concentrating her efforts on enumerating an unremitting list of the puppy's alleged transgressions in a bewailing, strident voice.

"HE JUMPS AND HE BITES!" Judy shrieks, clearly expecting me to gasp in dismay at this horrifying revelation.

"That's normal," I nod impassively. "That's how puppies play. There are some things—"

"BUT WE DON'T WANT HIM TO!" Judy howls in the way a spoiled child does when her new toy fails to perform as expected. "And Alan gets scared and cries when Midas bites him."

Barking Up the Right Tree

Tender Alan, meanwhile, is trying to catch poor Midas, who is doing his best to avoid him. Not a chance. Alan hoists Midas up in a bear hug and the squirming puppy is now biting half in fear and half in play. Alan drops the puppy on the tile floor and buries his head in his mother's lap, giving a heart-rending performance of having been mortally wounded, while Judy is swatting Midas on the snout yelling, "NO BITING!"

I do not have a reputation for suffering fools gladly and I've had enough. Enough of the caterwauling, enough of that vile child and its half-witted mother and enough of the capitals. The only reason I don't throw them out is because I still have some hope that I might alleviate the puppy's fate. Secretly cursing the veterinarian who referred them to me, I put to good use my classical voice training.

"Both of you, LEAVE THE PUPPY ALONE, and Alan, SIT DOWN!" I bellow, because I've got a few capitals of my own. With proper breath control, I can blow their eardrums out! Judy's mouth snaps shut audibly, whereas the boy's is as gaping open as his eyes. He plops himself on a chair, sulking. At this point I don't really care if they take their deplorable puppy and their injured feelings and depart. If I want to help Midas (for that is how I view the problem now), I must cut through this revoltingly overwrought display of the-puppy-toy-is-broken fix-it!

"It is perfectly normal for puppies and young dogs to jump, bite and chew," I explain, motioning imperiously to forestall any further emotional interruptions. "That is how they play." This should be obvious, but with these two dunderheads I take nothing for granted. "There are some ways I can teach you to redirect all that puppy energy onto a toy while you are playing with Midas. And Alan, he doesn't mean to hurt you, but if you are playing too roughly or wildly, Midas may still jump at you and chomp on you a bit; you'll survive that, won't you?"

Alan swallows and nods, eyes wide. Under raised eyebrows I fire a warning glance in his mother's direction to keep her from meddling.

"And you must not pick Midas up anymore. He is not a toy. It frightens him and he doesn't like it. Instead, you'll call him to you, and then you'll give him a treat. I'll show you how, okay?"

Alan nods while his mother is preparing to let out another burst of upper-case utterances.

No way will I allow her to part the floodgates again. "Let's go to the training field," I say quickly before Judy can open her mouth.

We begin by showing Alan how to play Puppy Fishing with Midas. This way he can play with the dog and keep a safe distance until he (Alan, not Midas) learns to be less frantic and petulant. Alan is almost having fun with this game, although he is a trifle maladroit and keeps getting the rope of the whip wrapped around his appendages. Midas pulls at the toy attached to the rope, and while Alan tries to disentangle himself, the puppy gnaws and nips at his hands in his effort to get the toy. Alan looks up, calculating on sympathy from his mother. When Judy rushes to set free her ill-fated offspring, I thwart her impulse by brusquely grasping her by her sweatshirt with one hand; with the other I wave at Alan.

"Good show, Alan!" I praise him, ostentatiously ignoring his plight.

Alan grins and continues to unsnarl himself while he is talking to Midas. Two puppies at play.

Next, we work on the Recall. First I show Alan how to

feed Midas from his flat hand, like a horse. Then I have Alan run away with treats in his fists, sending Midas after him. In his enthusiasm, Alan forgets my salutary advice and Midas bites the boy's fingers in his attempt to get to the treats. Alan returns with a pout and a face that indicates that the slightest display of maternal pity would result in a tearful downpour. Judy flounces off, anxious to sweep her mangled child into her arms.

"Not so fast!" I step in front of Judy. "I'll talk to him; you say nothing!" Yielding to my subtle persuasion, she nods.

Casually I question Alan, "You didn't feed him from your flat hand, did you?" When the boy shakes his head, tears close to the surface, I show him once more how to do it correctly and send him running off again, giving him no excuse to become lachrymose. This time Alan's travails are crowned with success and he returns with shining eyes and flushed cheeks, Midas on his heels.

"When he—when Midas—I gave him the food like this," he pipes breathlessly, stretching out his little none-too-clean hand.

"Oh, Alan, that is so wonderful," croons his mother in a honeyed voice.

Good grief, the woman is exasperating! Actually, the child isn't so bad once you get him away from his mother, who treats him like a dim-witted three-year-old.

But I haven't finished with Alan yet. "Let's do it again," I suggest, ignoring his mother.

"Yeah," nods Alan. Spurred by his success, he is demonstrating a modicum of enthusiasm at last.

This time Midas pushes Alan over. For a second the boy considers crying, but quickly abandons the idea and feeds the puppy. I once again have to restrict Judy from hastening to her darling's support.

Puppy Plight and Tyke Trouble

"He's okay," I reassure her. "We're dealing with a puppy, Judy, not a wild animal. Your son is ten times as big as Midas—he'll probably get more hurt playing with his pals or falling off his bike."

"Mmmh," says Judy, and it occurs to me that Alan might have neither bicycle nor friend. He certainly acts like it.

Their homework assignments include calling the dog with food, feeding him from their flat hands, playing Puppy Fishing, and in Alan's case, not to pick up, hug, or pursue Midas under any circumstances. Alan must not be left unsupervised with the puppy. Judy is not to commiserate with Alan when he is crying, but instead should separate child and dog for at least two hours, without display of emotion. Otherwise, she is not to come between Alan and Midas unless copious amounts of blood are flowing.

The following week there is much improvement in Alan and Midas' interaction, mostly due to Alan having changed his attitude considerably.

"It was really difficult not to interfere," Judy admits. "I wasn't always successful," she adds, now appearing almost reasonable.

"But on the whole, you did pretty well, judging by Alan's behavior," I condescend, saving my more enthusiastic approbation for the boy.

Alan is eager to show off. "Can I call Midas?" he asks impatiently.

We repeat the exercise until the puppy is tired and Alan's chubby little legs can't run anymore. This time there are no tears or emotionally charged scenes.

"You kept getting tangled up in the Puppy Fishing toy last week," I tell him, "so I made you a smaller one, just for you. Let's go and get it."

Barking Up the Right Tree

Alan is pleasantly surprised. "For my own?" he squeaks, reaching for my hand as he trots beside me to fetch the toy. He has evidently decided that I am not an ogre, after all.

"No, not a bad kid at that," I am thinking to myself.

"He still isn't housebroken!" Judy's whining slices through my charitable ruminations.

I presume she is talking about Midas. Forcing my voice to stay calm, I inquire after the methods Judy has used to housebreak Midas.

"Well, I rub his nose in his mess and I swat him on his behind, but he's not learning. I think he does it just to spite me. He gets angry when we don't play with him or leave him at home alone," Judy clamors.

I am gritting my teeth while listening to Judy. Everything the dog does is somehow wrought with sinister motives and directed at her or her child. A psychologist would have a field day with this character.

"Did you used to rub your son's nose in his mess?" I inquire, anticipating that this thought must disgust her, as it should.

"No!" Judy shakes her head vigorously as her eyes widen in alarm at the very idea of having her Motherhood questioned.

Good! "And did you assume that Alan messed in his diapers, or wherever, in order to deliberately irritate you?" I go on relentlessly.

"No, of course not, he was just a baby, he—well, sometimes I thought he was just being naughty," Judy replies with a nervous giggle.

Poor Alan. Having abandoned any last pretense of subtlety or decorum, I exclaim, "It is a cruel and perverted way to try to teach a puppy! No wonder he is so wary of you!"

Puppy Plight and Tyke Trouble

Although not even magnanimous souls would deem me excessively genteel or demure, I am nevertheless not customarily so high-handed or in the habit of venting my spleen on my clients. Not unless I have a perfectly good reason, that is. I deliberately pushed Judy and Alan past their typical comfort levels in order to quell the incessant display of extreme agitation. In addition, I succeeded in encouraging Alan to run and play until he was too tired to make much of a show of his misery. If there had been a way, I would have physically exhausted Judy also. Risking losing Judy as a client would not have overly burdened me.

"Well, I didn't know what else to do," comes the diffident reply.

"All right. Let's hope there is not too much damage to fix it. You can't force housebreaking on Midas; you have to facilitate it. His innate cleanliness will do the rest. Prevention is the name of the game. Until he is reliably housebroken, you must never leave him unsupervised. If you can't watch him, put him outside. You have to take him out first thing in the morning and thereafter every two hours. Take him out *before* he has an accident. If, through your inattention, he should have an accident anyway, ignore it. In addition—"

"What do you mean ignore it? I shouldn't clean it up, or I shouldn't punish Midas?" Judy interrupts anxiously.

I can't be sure, but I don't think this question was an uncharacteristic attempt at humor on Judy's part.

"Er—don't punish him. Punishing after the fact, even if it is right after the alleged misdeed, has nothing to do with training. By all means, clean up the mess. Furthermore, you have to let him out after each nap and after each meal and before you go to bed. At night—"

"At night we crate him in the laundry room," Judy cuts

in, "but he often doesn't make it through the night."

"So, because you don't want to be disturbed, you condemn Midas to lie in his own excrement," I chide her, making no secret of my disgust. "It's unfeeling and certainly no way to teach him to be clean."

"He could be crated in Alan's room at night," Judy suggests hopefully.

"Alan won't wake up when the puppy stirs. You know that children sleep very soundly," I spell out what should be obvious. "I suggest that you crate Midas in your bedroom, and when he fusses, tell him to be quiet. If he continues to be restless, he probably has to go. Take him outside. Don't play with him, don't talk to him a great deal, simply put him outside. When he relieves himself, praise him briefly and then crate him again. If he does not relieve himself and starts to play, as puppies are wont to do, ignore him and put him back in his crate. You don't want to teach him that he can wake you up for playtime. The first couple of weeks you may have to get up a few times per night, but it is well worth the effort."

Judy makes a face. "My husband won't like it, but I guess I'll have to do that."

Why this family ever got a dog, I cannot imagine. Clearly, the romantic idea appealed to them a great deal more than the reality. It seems to me that a great many people put quite a bit more energy into researching the purchase of a car or a TV than they expend on finding out what it requires to own a dog responsibly.

When Judy and Alan return two weeks later their frame of mind has improved noticeably. Even Midas is less agitated and he seems to enjoy Alan's company a little more. At least he is not evading the boy when he reaches for him.

Puppy Plight and Tyke Trouble

Setting black-and-white guidelines allows Judy and even Alan to gain control over the situation without getting overly emotional. The rest of the training goes relatively uneventfully, although the handler's sensitivity to the animal, which allows the interaction between human and dog to be finely tuned, is predictably lacking.

When Midas comes to our kennel to board, he shows himself as a reasonably well-adjusted dog. He has acquired a certain degree of independence and selective deafness, pointing to benign neglect, which, under the circumstances, is probably beneficial for him. Alan has evidently moved on to other interests, as one might expect.

Don't Fence Me In

Large and boisterous dogs and elderly, inexperienced own-ers are usually not a good combination, because all too often the needs of neither are met.

Dorothy and her husband Charles have brought me their one-year-old Dobermann bitch Shred. According to my first impression, this dog is a somewhat odd choice for them. Dorothy is a petite elderly lady, very soft-spoken, and al-though I sense a great deal of inner determination, I also guess that she has difficulty being firm with her dog. Her husband Charles is genteel with a friendly, somewhat vague demeanor. Shred, on the other hand, is a very overweight, unruly, and rather large, reddish-brown Dobermann. She has the soul of a long-distance runner, but because of her obesity, she lacks stamina. After a few short running spurts she putters around for a while, ignoring her owners com-pletely. When Dorothy approaches her, Shred does not try to avoid her touch, but her lack of interest is evident. Clearly, on Shred's List of Fascinating Pastimes, interacting with Dorothy and her husband ranks somewhere at the bottom.

I just have to ask. "What on Earth made you get a young Dobermann?"

"Well," Dorothy smiles, "a friend of ours is a plastic sur-geon, and when we decided to get a dog we asked him which breed, in his experience, caused the least damage. He stated that in over thirty years he never had to sew anybody up from the bite of a Dobermann, but that he had treated doz-ens of cases of nasty bites to hands and face from Golden

Retrievers and Labradors."

This corresponds with my experience. The Dobermann and certain other breeds have received an undeservedly bad rap, as much as Golden Retrievers and Labradors have earned an unmerited glowing image. The days, around the turn of the last century, when Mr. Dobermann created the breed "to challenge man or devil" are fortunately long gone. Nowadays, contrary to urban folklore, the Dobermann is a stable, vivacious companion (with a few exceptions, as there are in any breed, of course).

Shred is friendly and even-tempered. And yes, she is quite energetic, as a young Dobermann is supposed to be.

"I've taught her to sit and lie down with treats, but we need her to calm down," Dorothy complains. "I let her run in the yard—we have a big yard—but then when she comes back in, she races around in the house in spite of that. She just never sits still. When we have visitors she won't stay down: She is all over them and they don't like it."

Repressing my first impulse to retort, If you want a calm creature get a cast-iron lawn dog or one of those colossal porcelain dogs by the fireplace, not a large, vivacious breed, I explain with admirable composure: "Dorothy, you can't command dogs to be calm, at least not for extended periods of time. If you order an excited or overwrought dog to lie still, it is tantamount to forcing a tight lid on a pressure pot. *Calmness comes from within.* Some dogs of innately low energy are naturally calm; others seem calm due to their obesity. With active dogs, the only healthy way to calm them down is accomplished by regular and frequent release of energy through exercise."

Dorothy shakes her head, fretting. "But I cannot take her on a walk. She drags me around; she is so much stronger than I."

Don't Fence Me In

Generally, I don't believe it a good idea to own a dog who is physically stronger than you are. But what can I do? Although at first glance this is not a match made in paradise, there is no way Dorothy in particular is going to give up Shred and get a less powerful dog. Yet she and her husband lack the resolute demeanor usually necessary to lead such a strong animal.

"You will have to learn to control her off-leash. Only then can you take her on walks where she can actually expend enough energy to be placid in the house. There is no way, in any case, that you can provide her with enough exercise when you walk her on-leash."

Dorothy looks doubtful. "Do you think it would be possible for me to control her off-leash? I live right next to beautiful open space and I could take her for a walk every day if I could trust her not to bolt after other dogs and to come when I call her."

I have never made a habit of beating around the bush and I am not going to start now. "Dorothy, it's not going to be easy. I fear Shred is almost too much dog for you. The basis for perfect control is an unfailing, instantaneous and speedy recall. Practically all other exercises are largely ornamental. Thankfully, she has a very easygoing disposition. Nevertheless, you will ultimately have to prove your authority to her. She may *like* you, but she has to learn that you are significant for her well-being, if not her survival. Right now she doesn't even take you very seriously."

Dorothy is sent home with the routine advice not to feed her dog unless Shred is willing to interrupt her playtime and come when called in the yard. There is the predictable lamenting and hand-wringing about starving the poor dog, which fails to tug at my heartstrings. My imagination falls short to comprehend what is so dreadful about making a dog come to get his food. If he would rather play than eat, so be it. It is inevitable that he will come to get his food when he is hungry enough. If an overfed dog chooses not to exert himself in the slightest, nor to change his behavior in order to procure nourishment for himself, there is no cause whatever for alarm, provided the dog is not ill.

The task to get Shred to accept and seek Dorothy's leadership is much more daunting than it seems at first glance. It is immediately clear that Dorothy's physical strength is no match for Shred's, her calm, quiet demeanor at odds with Shred's exuberant nature. Therefore, it is not feasible for her to exert even modest pressure on the dog to compel compliance after the motivational teaching phase of training is completed. The idea of Dorothy yanking a leash or hurling Thor's Chain is unimaginable. Fortunately, it is possible to compensate for these deficits of strength.

It is a much more profound complication that Dorothy is unable to run and play vigorously with her dog. As far as our canine companions are concerned, we humans are simply peculiar dogs with impaired communication skills. The more we are able to approximate the dog's natural body language of social interaction (even at the risk of appearing a bit silly), the more attractive and comprehensible we can become to our dogs. Long before food or toys became the positive motivators of choice, a skilled dog trainer, or even an intuitive, animated dog owner, was able to draw his dog to him simply with the appropriate body language and the prospect of a little exuberant game as a reward.

In the case of training rewards, unquestionably, if some is good, more is better. The expectation of food and toys works better than either alone. The game of running after the owner, together with a bit of roughhousing or chasing a toy when the dog catches up with him, or the expectation of eating many delicious morsels while being stroked and scratched and addressed in a cheerful voice, or any random combination thereof works better than any of the elements alone.

Not surprisingly, Shred had not been conditioned to be exuberant and passionate about a toy, because her owners wanted her to be calm. In the case of Dorothy and Shred, this means that the food motivation alone has to be so strong that the dog is prepared to maintain a change in behavior.

In the following few weeks there is little significant change. Dorothy's yanking the leash to convince Shred that she *must* lie down more resembles a fly being tugged about on a rubber band than effective dog training. Therefore, Dorothy learns to compel the Down with the aid of a pinch collar and this works reasonably well. However, once off the leash, Shred has many absorbing pastimes to pursue and responding to Dorothy's feeble calls is not one of them.

Dorothy looks at me pleadingly. "She does now sometimes come in the yard. Well, once or twice, after that she loses interest."

Needless to say, Shred hasn't lost a great deal of her blubber, although Dorothy swears she is only feeding her when she responds to her call. I find this hard to believe.

"You absolutely must not feed her except when Shred is willing to interrupt her playtime. Calling her when she has nothing better to do and then rewarding her will only slow down the process."

"Still? Oh dear! I don't know if I can do that," Dorothy dithers.

My forbearance is wearing thin. "Look, Dorothy, I have no hidden solutions up my sleeve. In your case, there is no plan B, unless you want to make her so plump that she can hardly move. Then she'd be calmer. You'd have a lot of company."

This is an opportunity for me to hop onto another one of my favorite soapboxes.

At least eighty percent of dogs I see at the kennel and in training are seriously overweight. Many are morbidly obese. The most onerous part of combating overweight or obesity in dogs consists of convincing the owner. It is a common occurrence in our kennel that owners bring in their grotesquely obese dogs, then proceed to solicitously instruct me on how much to feed them. The amounts are often enough to choke an ox. At my innocent glance and tactful query of why they are feeding so much when their dog looks as if he were going to explode any minute now, my clients react mostly with disbelief or denial and the more or less snippy assertion that their vet thinks the dog is just fine.

Well, in my locale at least, there seem to be more vets than dogs and the competition is fierce. Many do not want to alienate their clients, although they know full well what the ideal weight should be and the dire consequences of obesity. *Feeding a dog to obesity is cruelty to animals.* Dogs are by nature runners and their bone and muscle structure is evidence of this. The amounts of food recommended on the dog food bags are frequently *more than double* what is necessary for a spayed or castrated pet kept indoors. Consider for a moment that in America dog food is a *six-billion-dollar-a-year* industry. If everyone fed only what is necessary or fed more healthful, fresh food, the industry would take billions in losses. *Of course* they want dog owners to believe that feeding a table scrap or a carrot or anything other than their dehydrated junk, which looks and smells like saw dust and dirt pressed into pellets, is not desirable. A diet replete with fresh, low-fat food is infinitely more healthful than the fat-laden kibble available in most feed stores. A number of good books on natural nutrition are available. *Dr. Pitcairn's Guide to Natural Health for Cats and Dogs* and Donald Strombeck's *Home Prepared Dog and Cat Diets*, both written by veterinarians, are two that come to mind immediately.

When viewed from above, dogs should not have the shape of a stuffed sausage, an egg, an eggplant or a bloated tick. They should have a discernible waist and an *hourglass* shape. The ribs should be palpable with your flat hand and only have the minutest layer of fat over them. From the side, the last rib should be visible, as should be a slight to moderate belly tuck-up, depending on the breed.

Several weeks later Dorothy returns with a very slim Shred. When she calls her in her small voice, Shred responds immediately.

"You were right," Dorothy says. "Once she was thin she changed her behavior completely. She comes now, every time. But now we have another problem. She steals food off the tables or counters."

"When you are there? She steals right under your nose or even food off your plate?" I ask. This could be a potentially serious problem of lack of respect.

"Oh, no! She doesn't really try it when we're there, and if she does I just call her away. But I can't leave anything on the counter and leave the room for very long."

It is hard not to sound patronizing when the solution is so simple. "Don't set yourself and Shred up for failure. Don't leave any food on the counter! It is not worth the battle; often the cure is worse than the disease. When you leave the room, in dog language you relinquish ownership. You have taught her to actively seek food and that's what she is doing.

When she was fat she had neither the energy nor the desire to exert herself for food."

"She's exerting herself now! She stole a big gingerbread man yesterday," Dorothy reports, half amused and half mourning its unorthodox demise. "And the day before—"

I am not going to take the bait. "You could strew a few rose petals on the counter or lay a wreath and hold a eulogy for the lamentable pastry, now resting in the belly of a happy Dobermann!"

"I'll keep the food off the counters when I'm not there," Dorothy nods with a resigned chuckle.

Next, we introduce Shred to the remote collar. As always in the beginning, it is set at a fairly low intensity as we take her into the marshlands. Shred is in heaven. Mice and gophers and ducks and other birds abound. Dorothy calls her and she comes to get her treat, but it is evident that the purchase power of doggie treats is no match for hunting real game. The recalls become less and less reliable. When Shred is engrossed in a particularly appealing smell, Dorothy calls her. Shred, as anticipated, pays no attention. Now I press the button on the transmitter for a split second. Shred is startled and jumps in the air with a little squeak, peering at the ground suspiciously. She evidently thinks that some creature just bit her. A samurai mouse, perhaps. Dorothy calls again and Shred hurries to her in search of security. She is praised and given a treat and sent off to play again. The next time she is inattentive she is "bitten" again, and once again she looks to find the invisible and fearsome culprit on the ground. But it must be dawning on her that higher powers are at work, because the third time she races to Dorothy without any delay. It would have been a grave mistake to punish Shred for the delay caused by her surprise. Once again, we must discern whether the dog is *unable* or *unwilling* to respond.

112

For the rest of the hour Shred comes as reliably as one might wish. The next objective is to convince Shred that the Holy Ghost is always on duty, everywhere. For the moment she associates only that she is "bitten" in case of disobedience in my marshlands. I am not quite ready to turn the electronic controls over to Dorothy. Too much could go wrong. Bad timing or bad judgment could destroy all the training efforts up to this point. There is almost no recovery from excessive or ill-timed compulsion.

The remote collar is an excellent training tool, but its very ease of use makes it susceptible to inappropriate application, as an instrument primarily of undeserved punishment rather than enforcing lessons the dog has already learned.

I am therefore not surprised when Dorothy asks hopefully, "Could I use the remote collar in the house?"

"For what?" I question her suspiciously.

"Well, you know, when she gets up on a counter or when she breaks her Down or when she jumps at a visitor."

"Absolutely, positively, irrevocably NO!"

"Oh!" says Dorothy, taken aback by my sudden vehemence. "But the little booklet that came with the collar says you could use it for all kinds of problems."

"Dorothy, these people want to sell. They clearly do not care that their collars could wind up in the wrong hands. If you start pushing the button every time you think Shred misbehaves, you soon will have a totally neurotic dog on your hands. Keep her and yourself sane and use it only when she refuses to return to you when you call her."

Dorothy does not give up easily. "But if she runs toward people to jump on them and she refuses to come, then I could use it?"

"Yes, indeed! That's one of the reasons why the recall has to be reliable. It is useful in so many situations. She cannot pursue an unauthorized activity if you call her away. Keep in mind, however, that you have to call her *before* she gets in trouble."

"I can do that!" Dorothy says as firmly as she is able. "I'll use the collar only for the recall."

Dorothy agrees to put the remote collar on Shred every time she lets her play in the yard. This way the dog is forming a positive connection with wearing the collar. It is to remain turned off. Under no circumstances is Dorothy to actually use the collar yet. For the next few days Dorothy increases the food rewards when Shred responds to her calls.

After a few days we are taking Shred out into the open space. Shred, properly dressed for obedience with her new remote collar, is elated. Apart from my marshlands, this is the first real walk she has taken. I need to remind her a couple of times that the Holy Ghost is on duty, but otherwise she responds speedily and reliably. Each time she comes to Dorothy, she is rewarded with a little pat, a few kind words, and intermittently, some treats. Being quickly released again to chase mice and gophers is for Shred the most important reward. Returning to her owner no longer means that her freedom is about to end.

For the next few days Dorothy needs to practice by herself. As almost always, this is cause for some anxiety for the owner and the trainer.

"Will she obey me?" Dorothy worries. "She knows and respects *you*, but will she respond to me?"

"Unless you want me to move in with you, Dorothy, you just have to take the leap. Everything is going to be fine. Call me tomorrow."

The next day Dorothy reports that she, too, had to summon the Holy Ghost a couple of times, but otherwise Shred maintained her conditioning.

Don't Fence Me In

A few months later Shred is in our kennel to board for a few weeks.

Since it is such a long stay, I occasionally take her for a walk in the marshlands in addition to her regular twice-daily group play. She responds willingly to my call and when I release her, she streaks off to chase some birds. Dorothy has obviously been doing a good job at maintaining Shred's obedience.

When Dorothy comes to pick up Shred I ask her, "So, how is it going for you and Shred? Are you still taking her for walks daily?"

"Yes," Dorothy smiles. "And everybody is commenting how calm she has become!"

Life With
the Schnauzer Family
Don't Leave Me Here to Cry!

Although I have occasionally separated the puppies for short periods of time from seven weeks of age, I now drastically increase the frequency with which this happens. More and more often now, I isolate one twin, from his sibling *and* from the other dogs, and spend one-on-one time with the other. Once training begins in earnest, there will be almost daily separation periods of about half an hour while I work with one of Schnauzers individually. There are two extremely weighty reasons for this.

First, I want both Ammo and Apache to bond to *me* more strongly than to each other. The ability to train them successfully irrevocably depends on this.

Secondly, if they are always together they will unquestionably develop less self-confidence than if they have to meet the world on their own terms, at least occasionally. In many cases, dogs who have been raised like Siamese twins become virtually dysfunctional when they have to be alone, even for very brief moments.

Today Ammo is the special puppy and is allowed to run errands with me. Like most dogs he loves riding in the car and barking contemptuously at the pitiful dogs who have to trudge by the side of the road while he is flying past them.

Some stores allow dogs, and even at the bank he is usually offered a biscuit. But then there are those moments when a reasonably well-behaved six-month-old puppy has to wait in the car.

I can hear the wailing from inside the supermarket. When I return to the parking lot, a small crowd has formed around my minivan. Ammo is having one of his temper tantrums and is screaming his bloody little head off.

Some of the perhaps well-meaning but rather misguided and meddlesome people in the crowd are trying to open my car, which I have wisely locked. (What on Earth would these people do if seventy pounds of bundled energy came flying at them?)

"He's not getting enough air," a woman caws rather idiotically, because several windows are partially open and it is a cool overcast day in January. Although in operas people sing and sing and sing while dying from tuberculosis or with a knife in their chest and stuffed into a potato sack, howling *this* loudly takes a lot of air. Ask any screeching soprano.

"Is this your dog?" The woman shoots me outraged glances from under her painted eyelids and stabs an accusing finger with a dangerously long, crimson-glittering nail at me. (What was she going to do? *Claw* my car open?) "It's a shame to leave him alone like that. You should never do that. He gets upset. I should report you," she squawks.

"Well, you see—" I begin with my customary placid affability, as people are staring. But of course, I can't get a word in edgewise. And why am I trying to explain anything to this presumptuous mooncalf at all?

"It's cruel," the woman continues her drivel. "I would never leave my dog alone like this. You should—"

I can't hear the rest, because I am driving away, Ammo licking my ears happily. Of course, it is people like this woman who pay me rather handsomely later on to ameliorate their dog's dreadful behavior problems.

Don't Leave Me Here to Cry!

I am not through yet with my little caterwauler. This time I park my car far away from civilization and go for a walk, alone. Ammo is furious and anxious and frustrated, and the howling starts once more with renewed vigor. After all, didn't it work last time? Howl in the car, and the old bat comes running to rescue her little Ammo-Whammo.

It won't work. This time he can howl until his nose bleeds and his vocal cords fray. His lung power is considerable and his vocal cords must be as thick and strong as steel ropes. At least while he is howling he is not taking the interior of my car apart.

After a seemingly endless time, which was actually only half an hour, the screeching subsides. Ten minutes later I return and we take a walk together. From then on Ammo occasionally howls for a few seconds when I leave, but that is the extent of his theatrics.

The Octopus

There is an element of subtlety in communicating with animals that cannot be learned. Some people show a great degree of sensitivity and intuition even with their first dog; their body language and tone of voice convey their message unfailingly. Others lack those same qualities, although they have owned (and sometimes even trained) many animals. Perhaps this phenomenon can be likened to the gift of musicality. Anybody can learn to play the piano or sing, but only the musically gifted are able to connect with the listener's soul.

When a dog has been raised in such a way that he is bonded and trusts his owner implicitly, training is usually a straightforward, enjoyable process. We teach the dog simple skills by making him believe that it is in *his* best interest to behave in a certain, conditioned, way. In the majority of cases that end up at my doorstep, however, it is necessary to repair the breach of trust between owner and dog before we begin the actual obedience training.

The strongest breaches of trust are created by acutely harmful attempts to change the dog's basic character or to eradicate species-specific innate behavior patterns. Attempting to turn a vivacious, enthusiastic dog into a Lovable Lump, a fiery dog into a Mellow Molly, or a Nervous Nelly into a Bodacious Bluto, to the unreliable degree that this can even be accomplished, exacts a terrible price from the dog. Likewise, to punish the dog for perfectly normal inborn behavior is harmful to the dog. Generally, dogs are less damaged by benign neglect than they are by misguided training attempts.

Barking Up the Right Tree

In my practice, problem behaviors are seldom due to cataclysmic events in the dog's life. Mostly, it is the subtle mistakes that eventuate a progressively widening rift between owner and dog. Initial mistakes, instead of being properly counterbalanced, result in further mistakes; error is heaped upon error and before long, with all the best of intentions on the owner's part, the dog's lack of trust in his owner's leadership is profound.

"He is driving us nuts!"

I perspicaciously infer Justin is referring to his young German Shepherd Dog mix, Abbot. Erica, his wife, is standing next to him nodding agreement. Abbot, meanwhile, is amusing himself on my training field, doing his level best to ignore or evade Justin and Erica.

When I ask Justin to approach him, Abbot nimbly stays out of reach.

"When I go after him, he runs away." Justin looks up and spreads his arms. "I don't know what to do anymore. I love this dog, but I don't think he's very bright."

"On the contrary," I declare, glancing at Abbot's wily fox face, "I think he's too smart for you!"

Justin is a likable chap and he doesn't take offense where none is meant, which, as I have had the opportunity to remark, is an absolute necessity when working with me.

Countless times I have heard owners tell me about their dog's intelligence or lack thereof. Inasmuch as one can speak of intelligence at all, the owners usually have it wrong. Exceedingly dull dogs, who have neither the energy nor the scope of inborn motor patterns to experiment with different options, are considered smart because they appear compliant. Reactive, enthusiastic, quick dogs, genetically programmed with an extensive range of different behaviors, are

The Octopus

considered stupid because their ability to discern very rapidly what is in their best interest, along with a strong sense of their own purpose, makes them appear defiant of clumsy training attempts.

Both Justin and Erica are, as so many of my clients, unaware that a deeper problem between them and the dog already exists. There are the usual attempts to keep Abbot from jumping. (Usually Abbot is jumping up at strangers, not at his owners, a sure sign that the dog prefers social interaction with strangers!) Mostly the instructions to the dog are so half-hearted and garbled that Abbot blithely ignores what seems to him incomprehensible or not in his best self-interest.

When Justin squats down to pet his dog, Abbot evades him, not fearfully, but he clearly does not want to be touched. Even when Justin feeds Abbot, the dog snatches the food, but turns around as soon as Justin reaches for him. And what does Justin do? Instead of letting the dog go, he lunges and grabs him. Abbot is not afraid, but he's plainly uncomfortable and wriggles free. Justin, meanwhile, is altogether unaware that anything has gone wrong at all.

Erica does not fare any better with her dog. When she bends down to touch Abbot, the dog avoids her. Like her husband, she now attempts to grasp her dog, who simply scurries back a little farther and strives to stay just out of reach. At my request, Erica feeds Abbot small pieces of treats. When I direct her to pet and praise her dog, she furiously paddles her hands about the dog's face as if she were trying to mess up someone's hairdo, chanting, "Goooood boyyy, goooood boyyy," in a piercing, never-varying singsong. Small wonder Abbot ducks away! Erica gets up with a pleased smile. She, too, is oblivious to the problem.

But *I* have to rub it in! "Abbot doesn't like you very much, it seems."

123

Barking Up the Right Tree

Before they can take exception I ask them to play with their dog. Both are stupefied for a moment, then look around searchingly for a toy. It is not hard to find a dog toy on my training field, and presently Justin picks up a tennis ball and throws it. Abbot—is anyone surprised?—ignores it completely.

"He plays with balls at home," Erica comments peevishly.

"At home there is not much else to do. If you are in prison, you watch the movie they are showing because it's better than nothing." (Never having been incarcerated, I hasten to affirm, my analogy is due to having watched too many old motion pictures.) I continue, "I'd like you to play with your dog, *without a toy*, not simply throw a ball."

Evidently, I have overtaxed those two. They look at each other, bewildered; then Erica gives me a beseeching smile.

No quarter given! "Go ahead!" I encourage them, waving my hands at them in a shooing motion.

Now follows a pathetic spectacle: Justin jogs and leaps about with his arms flapping, like an injured pigeon, shouting, "Abbot, Abbot!" and Erica zigzags with outstretched arms to snatch the alarmed Abbot, as one might endeavor to seize a defiant turkey designated for Thanksgiving dinner.

It is amazing how many dog owners do not have the faintest idea of how to play with their dogs. Their whole repertoire consists in throwing a toy and expecting the dog to retrieve it. How dreadfully boring this must be to both owner and dog.

My generosity of spirit demands that I put an end to this agonizing display. "That's enough." I wave my hand.

Relieved, the two approach. They still do not have a clue that anything is wrong. After all, they came to train their *dog*.

"You've got a problem," I tell them, nodding sagely.

The Octopus

"Your dog is hand shy and doesn't trust you."

"But—" says Erica.

"Yeah," drawls Justin.

Aha! Justin is the one I'll engage first. "You noticed, I am sure, that Abbot avoids your hand and when he comes to you he circles at arm's length, didn't you?"

"Yeah, that's right, he does that a lot," says Justin slowly.

"I don't think he's hand shy. He lies on the couch in the evening, and then I can pet him," Erica chatters. "His attention is diverted here; there are so many good smells and—" she fades out.

Erica clearly does not want to understand, and I find her vague, syrupy demeanor irritating. Of the two, she is the less talented one (if one can speak of talent at all).

"Although there are some exercises both of you can do, generally, it is better if the dog is taught first by one person, and then, when he comprehends, a second person can step in. It doesn't really work well if you switch back and forth, as in, 'Here, honey, you try for a while.' Justin, you seem to have a little easier time with Abbot, so I recommend that you stick with the training for the next few weeks."

Erica and Justin now engage in a tedious discussion concerning the logistics of training their dog. "You're at home more," Justin commences. "You should train him."

"Yes, that's true," Erica smiles, "but he already minds you better than me; you should train him."

Justin demurs, "All the more reason that you should work with him—"

And so on. We could be here all day and I'm getting a trifle bored; it is time for an infusion of my typical savoir- faire.

"Justin, we'll start with you!" I cut in briskly. "The fact that you have a little easier time with Abbot gives us a better start."

Barking Up the Right Tree

First, I instruct Justin not to reach for his dog under any circumstances. Fortunately, Abbot is slim and fit and a voracious eater. We begin with the first phase of the Rocket Recall. I hold the dog by the collar, while Justin runs off with his pockets and hands full of food. Abbot arrives and is rewarded with treats. Justin now restrains Abbot with both arms, in an attempt to hug him, I surmise. The dog squirms out of his clutches and bolts away. Justin leaps to his feet and tries to grasp him again.

"Stop! Stop!" I shout. "Leave him alone! You descend on him like a bloody octopus."

"A what?" Justin asks, cocking his head like a nervous bird.

"Oh, never mind. The point is that your hugging and grasping him makes him exceedingly uncomfortable, maybe even a little frightened. You activate his opposition reflex."

"You mean he pulls back?" Justin translates.

"Let me demonstrate!" I grasp Justin by the arm and drag him toward me. Reflexively, he braces himself. Now I push him by the shoulder and again, as expected, he does not topple, but resists my shove.

"It's an automatic response. All higher organisms have it and for all I know, the lower ones do, too. I want you to concentrate on not drawing him to you with your hands. Hold the food in such a way that Abbot has to make body contact with you if he wants to eat. Let's try it again!"

Justin runs away once more with the food and Abbot follows.

As soon as Justin attempts to pet his dog, however, Abbot again jerks away and hesitates at arm's length.

As before, Justin reaches for his dog, but this time I bellow, "Don't *reach*, damn it!"

Justin's hand twitches back and he grins at me apologetically. "Sorry, I forgot."

We repeat the exercise and this time Justin controls himself for ten seconds and *then* he reaches for his dog. Abbot jumps back.

I leap up, abandoning for the moment my accustomed poise. "Imagine, if you will, that your elbows are tied to your belt and you cannot move forward, only back up."

Justin nods, "Yeah I know—"

"Maybe I could tie your arms to your belt with this leash," I offer helpfully, giving Justin my sweetest smile.

This worries him. "No, that's all right, I can do it," he mumbles, and I swear he is blushing.

"Pardon?"

Justin clears his throat. "I can do it," he repeats more audibly.

Let us leave Justin and his embarrassment alone for a moment while I explain.

Most animals, including dogs and humans, do not appreciate being grasped or what they may consider the threat thereof. They view the thrusting of a hand in their face as an act of exceedingly poor manners, if not outright hostility. A dog's olfactory sense, as most everyone knows, is exponentially better developed than ours; he can smell us very well many yards away (and of course, also perceive us visually).

At the kennel, we have a client who is convinced that she can improve her attractiveness by bathing in a heavily cloying perfume. After she leaves, I can smell the lingering cloud of her fragrance in our *parking lot* for half an hour— much longer in the office. And like a dog who can scent us very well indeed, even from a distance, I certainly do not wish her hand to be shoved under my nose for purpose of identification, or any other purpose, for that matter. I, like the dog, would be tempted to bite it.

It is much more polite, not to mention infinitely safer, to coax the strange dog and *let him come to us*. When he seeks out our hand, *then* we can stroke, or preferably scratch him a little, without reaching for him when he backs up. Some dogs tolerate being reached for, none like it, and a few will take offense.

Justin and Erica's assignment consists of playing Puppy Fishing, playing with two balls, and calling Abbot with food. Barring emergencies, neither he nor Erica are to reach for the dog for any reason. They must feed him in such a way that the dog must make prolonged body contact if he wants to eat. When they pet him they are to stroke and scratch; they must pay heed not to stroke Abbot across the eyes; under no circumstances are they to pat Abbot, particularly on his head. Since the dog also resists having his collar slipped over his head, I advise Justin to hold collar and treat in such a way that the dog has to stick his head through the collar in order to get the food.

The next few weeks show a gradual improvement of the relationship between Justin and Abbot, although it takes countless reminders for Justin not to restrain his dog with his hands. Erica comes along to the training sessions, but mostly smiles and observes. Abbot begins to enjoy being with Justin and responds well to the recall most times, although the slightest threat of being grasped still causes him to scurry away.

I dismiss Justin and Erica with the exhortation to continue practicing. Justin is to help Erica by reminding her to be less intrusive with her hands. When the problems with Abbot's avoidance behavior have abated, they need to come back for further sessions to secure the obedience and make it reliable.

The Octopus

After about four or five months Justin and Erica return with Abbot, with the usual complaint that Abbot is developing rather selective hearing. Justin learns to enforce the recall with the Thor Chain reasonably successfully, although the dog is still somewhat suspicious and not completely comfortable with prolonged body contact after having been called. Both complain that Abbot does not obey Erica at all, even when she uses treats. Indeed, Abbot does everything he can to avoid Erica's inept attempts at interaction. There is just no question about it: He does not trust her and he does not particularly like her. I almost feel sorry for Erica. Almost. Even though I believe that she has never treated Abbot harshly and I can see that her efforts are well-meaning, there is something about her vague, saccharine demeanor that makes me, too, want to stay away from her. Indeed, it is embarrassing to see how Abbot always greets me like a long-lost friend, landing in my lap and seeking body contact. If I took him away he would go with me happily, never looking back. The much-vaunted unconditional love and loyalty that dogs are supposed to have exist mostly in their owner's romantic imagination. I know many dogs who would file for divorce if they only could.

Erica's persistent difficulties in her relationship with her dog result in her inability to wield any control over Abbot. This is an unsafe situation for both of them, unless Erica completely relinquishes any aspirations that Abbot will ever obey her when he is not on a leash. In light of being faced with this seemingly insurmountable obstacle and in my desire to help Erica *and* Abbot, I now let wishful thinking supersede my practical experience as well as my powers of reason.

Teaching Erica to use the throw chain would be an exercise in futility, because of Erica's poor sense of timing, her vexing show of simpering ineptitude, her shaky relationship with her dog and Abbot's adroitness at staying out of reach. Therefore I seek to enforce the recall by way of the electric remote collar, although I should have been aware that no force in the world could make a dog come reliably to an owner whom he does not trust. At the lower levels of intensity, Abbot ignores completely the little sting he feels. Even at gradually higher levels of stimulation, most of the time he would rather feel discomfort or mild pain than come to Erica.

I use this approach in one session only. Fortunately, his owners, who truly have only the best in mind for their dog, decline to proceed with this ineffective and, under the circumstances, inappropriate method. I have no choice but to admit partial defeat, sending Erica and Justin home with the advice to continue using treats.

The Spoilsport

Most dog owners have learned that it is a grave mistake to punish their dogs when they come to them, even if the arrival is somewhat tardy. What they fail to recognize is that restriction of freedom and end of playtime can also be considered a form of punishment.

Daisy, the white Terrier-Shepherd mix, is way ahead of her owner; she scampers up the dog walk and proceeds on the level part with considerable speed, while Linda is giving her best effort to keep up with her. As she descends the obstacle Daisy waits obediently and eagerly for a moment, her tail wagging, her pointy nose expectantly in the little pot we have placed there as a receptacle for the food rewards. When she finds no treat, she hops off the dog walk and bounds to greet her owner, who by now has caught up with her.

"I'm getting too old for this," gasps Linda, bent over, her hands braced on her knees. Her dog Daisy is prancing around her and trying to get Linda to resume the agility training.

"Nonsense!" I chide her. "You don't have to be that fit for agility, you just have to control your dog and get your timing right. Control you've got, now we work on your timing. You are running way too much. You could, for instance, cut across here between the oxer and the tunnel; you don't have to take the long way around."

"I guess I can't run and think at the same time," Linda puffs.

The next attempt is much more successful and Linda

and Daisy reach the contact zone at the same time. When Daisy waits and points to the target with her nose, she is rewarded with treats and then released.

Linda is proud of her dog. "What a good girl," she bends down and praises her enthusiastically, while Daisy jumps up to maximize the benefit. "Do you remember what you said to me when I first came to you for training?" she glances up at me. Before I can answer she goes on, "You said, 'I don't know if I can help you!'"

How well I remember! Linda was waiting for me in front of my office as I came trotting off the training field, marginally late for the appointment as usual.

"There's a dog in the office and Daisy isn't very good with other dogs. Can we do the evaluation outside?" Linda asked after the introductions were made.

"Surely. Let's go to the training field."

In her owner's and my presence Daisy showed herself to be a shy, rather submissive creature. Away from her owner, however, her confidence rose dramatically. This is always a very bad sign. When Linda called her dog, Daisy quickly put more distance between herself and her owner and when Linda tried to approach, Daisy ran away.

(As I have mentioned before, my training field with the adjoining marshlands, all fenced in, is large enough to give a dog the illusion of freedom.)

At my request, Linda turned and ran in the opposite direction. Daisy made no attempt to follow, even at a distance.

When we left the training field, Daisy did not look up at the sound of the closing gate. From my office window we could observe Daisy as she amused herself, not a worry in the world. She was completely unconcerned that Linda might be on a rocket ship to the moon by now.

After some thirty years of dealing with dogs and their owners, I can discern a problem owner every bit as fast as I can a problem dog. Linda did not fit into the category of problem owner. She was smart and sensible, did not take herself overly seriously, and appeared fairly decisive. (Nothing is more difficult to understand, from a dog's point of view, than a vague or muddleheaded person.) Her demeanor was open and refreshingly unpretentious.

"You've had Daisy since she was a puppy?" I was looking for excuses.

"No, actually —"

Oh good. That must be it, an inherited problem!

"— actually, I got her when she was about four months old," Linda concludes.

Damn! There went that hope. My uneasiness was not only the result of apparently having lost my flair for assessing owners, it also came from understanding that it is often very difficult for those who have *caused* some or all of the dog's problems to facilitate their solution.

Although it is not always possible to surmise what exactly went wrong in the rearing of a dog, I believe at least part of the battle is won when the owner and I have a clearer understanding of where the mistakes were made.

"I take it Daisy is never off-leash?" I continue my fishing expedition.

"Not unless she bolts out of the door, which she still manages to do occasionally. When that happens she is usually gone for the better part of the day. I don't take her on walks on-leash much anymore, because she is so aggressive when she meets other dogs."

The old story: problem behavior made worse by constant confinement and lack of strenuous physical activity.

"She didn't used to be this aggressive with other dogs. When I lived near the beach she went out for a run every day and was fine with dogs she met," Linda went on.

"On leash?" I ask.

"Oh, no! I would just let her out the front door and she'd take herself for a run, then come back an hour or two later."

I had slumped in my seat, but now I was bolt upright. "That's your problem! How long did this go on?"

"A couple of years maybe. I wish I still lived at the beach so I could give her more freedom, but I have to be closer to my work. The commute was killing me."

"There's your problem," I repeated. "By letting her find out that she does not need you to have a good time, you have relegated yourself to the role of party pooper. When she is with you, she is confined, or you threaten to confine her. Her behavior does not please you and of course she can feel that. When she is alone, she is free of stress and she can go and play."

Linda was confused. "But after we moved away from the beach and before she got so aggressive, I would take her on a walk every day."

"On leash?" I asked, although I could guess the answer.

When Linda nodded I asked her, "You don't call a leash confinement?"

Linda hesitated for a moment. "You know, I've never even thought about a leash as confinement. Isn't the leash supposed to be a good sign for the dog, because she is about to go on a walk?"

"A walk on a tether *is* confinement. I suppose walking around in a circle in a prison yard is better than not walking at all, but it isn't the real thing."

"I'm beginning to see what you mean," Linda said slowly.

The Spoilsport

"Dogs who are always confined *will* develop neurotic behavior, partly because of the confinement itself and partly because there is no way to provide enough exercise for a dog on leash, unless you run him alongside a bicycle, which is boring."

"But I can't let her run off leash, because I can't control her," Linda stated.

"Precisely. If we can get her to respond to you off leash, and that's a big if, the rest of the problems—the bolting out of doors, the aggression towards dogs—are minor problems and can be controlled. If she bolts out of a door, for instance, you simply call her back."

"Oh, wouldn't that be nice," Linda said.

We began by attempting to motivate Daisy to come to Linda by using treats. Daisy had not been conditioned at an early age to love balls or toys; therefore, using treats as a positive motivation was our only alternative. Not surprisingly, Daisy chose freedom over food.

Now, Daisy in those days was far from the relatively slim and fit dog she is today. In fact, she was rather roly-poly.

I advised Linda not to feed Daisy anything except treats from her hand when she came to her in her yard or on a Flexi-line out in the park.

"Daisy may go on a hunger strike for several days, maybe a week or more. I don't want you to cave in to her. If she wants to eat—"

"A week!" Linda's eyes widened in dismay.

"Or more," I continued unperturbed, as I am used to these outbursts of misplaced kindness to animals. "If she wants to eat she has to come. It's our only hope. Compulsion at this stage would only make the problem worse," I admonished Linda, extracting the promise to follow my directions assiduously.

Barking Up the Right Tree

Week after week I checked Daisy's progress, which as expected was very slow, as was her weight loss. Daisy was understandably reluctant to trade in her perceived freedom for food—food her body did not really need.

"How much do you give her when she comes to you?" I asked Linda.

"About this much," Linda indicated a large handful.

"No wonder! You're undermining your own efforts. From now on Daisy is to get about this much when she comes," I said, indicating a thimbleful. "And that amount has to be broken down into several pieces, which you must feed one by one."

After about four months in which there was slow but steady progress, I felt confident enough to introduce Daisy to the power of Thor. To all appearances this worked very well and I sent Linda off to practice in safe and fairly distraction-free environments for a couple of weeks. We concluded the training by successfully securing the Drop at a Distance.

Finally, the big day arrived. We would take Daisy hiking to a rather popular part of the wooded open space where we were sure to meet many people walking their—often not very well controlled—canine companions.

For the first half-hour Daisy was a paragon of successful training. Linda had to summon Thor once at the beginning of the walk, but after that Daisy was as obedient and controlled as anyone might wish. She stayed near, came immediately when called, particularly *before* she ran up to other dogs. When given permission to go ahead, she greeted other dogs in a non-aggressive, if somewhat submissive, fashion.

Quite unexpectedly, however, Daisy bolted away toward another dog farther down the trail, and even when Thor hurled his flash of lightning at her rear she kept going. A glitch but nothing serious, or so I thought.

The Spoilsport

"Just let her go; she'll come right back," I declined the helpful hiker's offer to restrain Daisy until we could get her.

But she didn't come right back. Quite to the contrary, as we approached she kept putting more and more distance between herself and us, and eventually she ran around a bend and out of sight. It appeared that all our efforts had been for naught. The old behavior had broken through the newly laid veneer of training with full force. We walked and walked. No sign of Daisy.

Linda became visibly upset, although she tried not to let it show. "At least at the beach she knew how to find her way back home," she agonized.

"No need to panic," I consoled her and amended in my mind, not yet, anyway.

But by now I was worried as well. Fifteen, twenty minutes had passed and still no Daisy. In this huge open space she could run for hours or she could head straight for the road. As we quickened our pace I tried not to think of it, but instead hitched my hope to the possibility that Daisy was exhibiting pre-extinctive behavior.

It is a curious thing, this extinction burst, as psychologists call it. When it occurs it always feels like someone is declaring war on my nerves by pulling the rug out from under my feet. Lulled into a sense of security and accomplishment because the training progresses smoothly, it comes as a mighty jolt when the old behavior surfaces with renewed intensity. The problem, of course, is that I cannot ascertain if the behavior is truly pre-extinctive until *after* it has subsided and the recently conditioned behavior has taken hold again. It is as if a reformed alcoholic goes on one last drunken binge, then kicks the habit forever.

It is absolutely imperative that the trainer not be drawn into this quagmire of emotions, but keep a cool head. This is not easy and requires a great deal of self-control, since the distress on the trainer's part is quite possibly even higher than the dog's.

As we were walking I explained this to Linda, partly to reassure her and partly to quell my own rising apprehension as we rounded another bend, and still no Daisy.

At long last we saw her standing in the middle of the trail looking lost and rather sheepish. Linda rushed to put her on leash.

"No, Linda," I said, holding her back, "that's just what she expects and what you have always done. Let her think if she does not come, you'll let her rot in these woods."

As instructed, Linda squatted down and called Daisy, just like she had done hundreds of times in training, without cajoling or begging. Daisy came immediately as if this whole frightening episode had never happened.

"Now can I put her on leash?" Linda asked.

"No, now we'll hike back as if nothing had happened, and by the time we arrive at the parking lot we'll know if we did the right thing!"

We walked the few miles back to the parking lot at a considerably more leisurely pace and that little devil Daisy was as obedient as before. I advised Linda to take Daisy to the same area the following day to see if the training maintained.

"I was scared witless when I took her out by myself that next day," Linda recalls, "but she has gotten better and better every day. There never was a recurrence of that dreadful episode. I take her hiking now nearly every day, she mostly stays at a distance of no more than thirty or forty feet and she is delighted to come instantly when I call her. And overall, she seems so much calmer and happier now."

The Spoilsport

The fact that dogs do become calmer and happier with appropriate bonding and training is a universal truth. Regular and frequent exercise, together with the knowledge of a few very simple rules, relieves the dog's stress effectively.

Agility training is over and even though her owner is exhausted, Daisy has energy to spare. She is running circles with Maggie, the Kerry Blue, and Callie the German Shepherd. All inappropriately submissive or aggressive behavior has disappeared and she is open and free in her interaction with people and dogs. It is impossible to see in this dog the former pathetic cringing and evasive creature she once was. However, when I see her, I will always be reminded of that sinking feeling we had when we took her for a walk in the woods.

Life With
the Schnauzer Family
Who's the Boss?

At six months of age, the Schnauzerkinder are almost as tall as their mother. Ilka still rules them with an iron paw. Although she is never really mean to them, it is unmistakable that she is in charge. Ammo in particular has a healthy respect for his mother. Indirectly, this makes my job rather easy, as both the Schnauzer twins recognize and accept benign authority readily.

Although all dogs are born with motor patterns that signal submissiveness and compliance, if these responses are not practiced when the dog is relatively young, they petrify. If a dog has made a habit of saying *I will not!* to his leader, it often is an irreversible problem. An aspiring dog trainer can learn infinitely more by observing a normal dog mother with her brood than by reading all the training books in the world.

Ammo has secretly climbed onto the bed, which I do not encourage, but occasionally tolerate. He is as proud as a pasha and eyes his surroundings suspiciously, lest his pesky sister might want to compete for this prime spot. This is hard work and Ammo dozes off.

Ilka has spied the open bedroom door and hops on the bed. Ammo—and there is a good reason for his name—explodes into a temper tantrum, roaring loudly, mistaking her for his sister. Ilka will have none of it. She simply growls sharply at her errant son with a mien of absolute authority.

141

Barking Up the Right Tree

Ammo is so shocked that his erstwhile roar modulates into a loud squeal, and then into a pitiful undulating howl as if he were begging for mercy for his foolhardiness. Ilka does not lay a tooth on him, but instead glares disapprovingly. Ammo cannot stand the pressure and leaves the bedroom with a disgruntled air.

The relationship of the Schnauzer twins with each other is quite another story. Their constant squabbles are a bit unnerving. Ammo tries tirelessly to assert his superiority. He is larger than his sister, but as boys are in adolescence, far less mature. I imagine their daily dialogue somewhat like this:

Ammo: Let's play.

Apache: Yeah! Good idea!

(They play for a minute.)

Ammo: You're just a girl. Let's play I'm the boss!

Apache: Ha! I'm a warrior and you're a schmuck! *I'm* the boss!

(Fight for five seconds. Sound and fury and spittle flying, but no damage.)

Ammo: Shit game! I'd rather catch a mouse.

(Trots off with wounded pride.)

As belligerent and competitive as the Schnauzer twins are with each other, with other puppies and adults they interact in a reasonable manner; therefore I am not worried. Later in life, when they are physically mature, they will refrain from carrying this rivalry to dangerous levels, because both are provided the protection of their sex. If I had chosen to have Ammo castrated, however, Apache might quite possibly regard him as serious competition. Likewise, had I chosen to keep two females or two males, this persistent struggle for superiority would be very worrisome.

Who's the Boss?

It is time to ascend one of my numerous soapboxes. Many half-truths and some outright nonsense about so-called neutering are bandied about by the ideologically zealous. The undeniable fact is that castration and spaying have a negative effect on physical development. Early spaying in the female often leads to lifelong incontinence, which can vary from mild to very messy. Altered animals, without doubt, have a tendency to become fat, or at the very least, they need considerably less food and more exercise to stay fit than they would if they were intact. Human castrati were known as having "an angel's voice in an elephant's body." Likewise, I do not have to turn a dog over to see whether he was castrated. The underdeveloped musculature and the mountain of fat carried on long, skinny legs and the disproportionately small head are hallmarks of this condition. It is a myth that most intact males are uncontrollably aggressive. Castration is never a substitute for proper socialization and training!

No lucid person would argue that canine birth control should not be taken very seriously. It does not have to be accomplished by mutilating perfectly healthy dogs, however. If the male dog needs to be sterilized, a vasectomy is a humane and benign alternative.

This castration mania we see today is an entirely American phenomenon. Most European veterinarians refuse to spay or castrate, unless there is a good medical reason for it. It is perhaps not surprising that this refusal to amputate healthy organs is prevalent in countries that also outlaw the maiming of dogs' ears and tails. I dream of the day when whittling a dog to order—barbarically cutting away what offends our sensibilities—becomes politically incorrect everywhere.

143

Every Search Dog Will Have Her Prey

Predatory behavior is an integral part in our dogs' psychological makeup. It cannot be eradicated, and any attempt to do so does great harm to the dog. It can be controlled, however, and channeled into constructive outlets.

"Your dog isn't much of a barker," Willy, our team leader, says disdainfully.

Most dog owners would not consider this pronouncement in any way undesirable. For me, however, it presents a substantial hurdle in training Schnupp, my Dobermann, as a search dog. In disaster areas, upon scenting a person in the rubble, she is supposed to alert her handler by barking and digging at the site.

"And what's worse, she is not very interested in balls or tug toys. She has to be fanatical about toys for search-dog training. Otherwise she's no good to us," Willy goes on heartlessly. "Or how else would we get her to hold the bringsel? Not to mention retrieve various items?"

In area searches a dog wears a small leather tab fastened to his collar. Upon locating the victim, the dog flips the so-called bringsel into his mouth and returns to the handler, thus indicating he has found the victim. Subsequently, the dog leads the handler back to the victim. Alerting the handler by barking in vast mountainous areas is not effective, because it may be difficult to pinpoint the sound correctly.

"I know, I know," I say, a little discouraged. "I only got

145

her as an adult; otherwise I would have developed her prey behavior and imprinted her on toys. She does have loads of prey drive, though. Before I got her she worked off her excess drive on chasing horses and the neighbor's chickens. However, now she mostly pursues mice and squirrels. You wouldn't be willing to put a mouse in your pocket when you hide to be the victim, would you?"

"No," says Willy.

"She is fanatical and pushy about food, that's something," I say hopefully.

"Well, it's a start," Willy concedes. "At least she's confident. Otherwise, I'd tell you to forget trying to make a search dog out of her. Go home and get her to bark for food. You can do that, can't you? You're a dog trainer, after all."

In fact, Schnupp does not hesitate to bark forcefully at the door or when she is protecting my car. The intruder-alert bark, however, is substantially different from the gimme-gimme prey bark. The bark I am trying to produce with Schnupp is not an aggressive bark, but the same excitedly happy bark she emits when she has treed a squirrel.

At home I tease Schnupp with her dinner. She is jumping around frantically, but she is not barking. I continue to let her sniff the food, then quickly withdraw it. For Schnupp, comestibles are *serious* business. She is quivering and drooling in her eagerness, but she is still not barking. Finally, when she looks like she might burst with frustration, in her excitement she spits out a sound. It hardly seems like a bark, but instantly I put her food down and let her eat.

The learning curve is steep. The next day, when I tease her with her food, she makes a tiny wuff sound. Immediately, I let her devour her dinner. The following day I hold out for two wuffs. Every day I let her bark a little longer, now giving the command *"Gib Laut!"* ("Bark!") *while* she is barking. After about two weeks, she barks heartily and happily for her food.

Clearly, Schnupp learned to bark on command *not from barking*, but from *achieving her goal*, in this case, eating. The "positive reinforcement" we hear about so often is nothing more than this: The dog gets what he wants or, more correctly, he gets what his *internal program dictates* he needs. Once his goal is reached, the learning connection is complete. It is completely ineffective to merely repeat an exercise a thousand times without letting the dog reach his biological goal, such as prey (food, toys) or physical or emotional well-being. It is equally absurd to punish a dog even mere seconds after he has stolen the sausage, for example. Once the sausage is in the dog's mouth, the mental association is concluded; the show is over and the credits are rolling. It follows that the dog must want something in order to learn and he must want it strongly enough to change his behavior in order to get it. It is difficult to teach an overfed, overly indulged, lethargic dog who wants for nothing.

"Well, let's see how well she alerts," says the ever-so-skeptical Willy when we return to search-dog training.

He teases Schnupp briefly with a choice morsel, then crawls into a structure specifically built for the purpose to teach dogs to dig and bark. It looks like a narrow tunnel leading into a hillock with a lid at the entrance. The lid has a slit window and a handle on the inside so the "victim" can open it at the appropriate time to reward the dog.

Schnupp knows that Willy and, what is more important, the food he carries are somewhere in the tunnel. She circles the hill and presently sniffs at the opening where the scent is strongest. The lid is closed.

Schnupp tries the easy way. She returns to me, looking

at me beseechingly. After all, I am the great master who can open doors, particularly the one to the cookie cabinet. So why not this one? Owners should be useful for something.

"Don't help her!" comes Willy's muffled voice from inside the contraption.

Schnupp, thoroughly disgusted with my refusal to assist her, has taken her station at the entrance of the tunnel again. She begins to dig frenziedly, but does not bark. She has not made the connection that barking at the tunnel is the same as barking for her dinner. Now I help her by giving her a command: "*Gib Laut!*" For two weeks she has heard this command *while* she was barking. And now the penny drops. Schnupp barks. Willy immediately opens the lid and lets her crawl into the tunnel to get her treat. Here too, the learning curve is very steep.

The objective to get Schnupp to work for toys is much more difficult. It is easy to make a dog hungry; however, withholding toys would not overly burden her, particularly as long as there are other things to do. How can I create a desire in her to chase objects?

In the evening Schnupp does not get her usual long walk. Early the next morning—well, relatively early—when it is still cool and Schnupp's energy is high, I take her out into the dog run. There are no mice or gophers there, no interesting smells, no canine playmates, a place for boredom and rest. But Schnupp is brimming with pent-up intensity; she wants to do *something*. Now even chasing the silly toy on the string allows for some purposeful activity. Before Schnupp's interest wanes, I leave her in her run. In the evening, once again, there is no extended walk. The following morning Schnupp immediately pursues the toy on the buggy whip. If there are no mice to hunt, well, what's a young Dobermann to do? In only a week, chasing toys on a string becomes a favorite activity. Now I can gradually move on to a variety of toys. After several months, although Schnupp still adores chasing mice, she would rather play ball or tug-o'-war with me. Now her training as a search dog can begin in earnest.

The Chase Is On

When a dog is very excited, his mental state is different from the one he is in when kept in a relatively distraction-free environment. He cannot be reached with the same type of communication that suffices when he is in a comparatively calm state of mind.

"Lexie needs some refresher training," Annette informs me on the phone. "Urgently! I can't take her on walks anymore. She just takes off after any dog she glimpses on the horizon, or anything else that moves, for that matter."

"She won't come back for treats or a ball?"

"Not at all," Annette snorts. "She just keeps running to the next thing that incites her interest. She comes fine for treats in the yard, but once she is out in the open space, forget it!"

"It won't be difficult," I promise Annette. "You prepared Lexie well with positive motivation. All she needs now is a little compulsion for reinforcement."

Lexie, a one-year-old German Shepherd bitch, had indeed gone through Puppy Playschool and, due to her energy and high drives, had shown herself to be an extraordinarily quick study. Now, however, it seems as if she had matured all of a sudden, as is so often the case. Inevitably, with increasing age, the world has opened up to her and she has become more independent. But I remember Lexie as guidable and receptive, without being overly sensitive—a very fine representative of her breed. She has been raised properly and supervised through her puppyhood with an effective mix of love and leadership.

Piece of cake, I think to myself. But I couldn't have been more wrong.

On my training field and in the marshlands, Lexie is distracted and rather sloppy in her recall, just as I had envisioned. Thor's Chain quickly sets this to rights.

"You see?" I grin. "Nothing to it. Tomorrow we practice it out in the open space, and once the recall is solid, the Down is going to be a snap."

"I hope you're right," Annette fusses. "You don't know what she's like once she is out on a walk."

I wave away her doubts grandiloquently. "Trust me! I'm usually right in these things."

Out in the open space, Lexie indeed bolts toward the first dog she sees moving in the distance. I'm not concerned— yet. Of course, I have seen the dog, too, and Thor is ready for her with impeccable timing. Nonetheless, Thor's Chain bounces off Lexie's behind while she keeps going as if she had merely been struck by a feather. When she meets up with the dog, she greets him obsequiously and continues to fawn and cringe until we pick her up.

"She is much too submissive for her age," I shake my head, frowning. "It doesn't seem to fit her overall disposition."

Well," Annette admits, "she hasn't met very many dogs since she was a puppy."

"Why not? I thought I explained to you that socialization is an ongoing process."

"You did, but you see why I can't take her off leash," Annette shrugs helplessly. "She's gone in a flash when she sees another dog or anything else in motion. She's such a pleasant easy-going dog at all other times, but when she sees something stirring, it's as if she were shifting into another mental dimension. I can't get through to her."

"Sometimes," I make light of Annette's concern, "Thor has to strike several times in a row before the point registers. She'll learn very quickly. You'll see. Let's try it again."

The same embarrassing scene, however, unfolds several more times. Lexie completely ignores the thrown chain and bolts toward her target, usually a running dog. There she fawns and cringes and does not return when called. Each time, we have to pick her up and physically remove her from the scene by her collar.

"No wonder she runs away from you when you throw chains at her," an irate busybody, walking (or I should say waddling) a morbidly obese Labrador, yells at us. "You should be using treats! Have you never heard of training a dog with love? Your dog should be on a leash, anyway."

Great! Just what I need right now! I was *so* hoping for a lecture from an ignoramus! How I loathe having to learn from my mistakes! Especially when the mistakes are witnessed by dozens of people.

"Hypertrophic prey drive," I mutter between clenched teeth.

"What?" Annette asks

"Excessively high predatory behavior," I explain. "Lexie's inborn drive to chase and hunt is so high that it takes very little to trigger the behavior. As her drive shoots up, so does her adrenaline. I think this makes her seem to shift into another mental realm. As a result of the adrenaline rush, her pain threshold also shoots way up. When she chases something the blood is singing in her ears and she is deaf to the world. That's why you can't get through to her and why she doesn't notice Thor's Chain. Once she arrives at her target, she of course knows it's another dog and she starts her appeasement behavior."

Barking Up the Right Tree

"Pretty bad, huh?" Annette asks dejectedly.

"No, not really. Now that I've finally figured it out, I'll stop underestimating her. On one hand, high prey drive is actually very useful and can easily be subverted to train the dog. This is the reason she learned so quickly when she was a puppy. Remember how easily she can be motivated with a ball or a toy or food—"

"Yeah, when there is nothing better to chase," Annette cuts in resentfully.

"Right. On the other hand, of course, we have to teach her to control her own behavior when appropriate."

"Like when I'm calling her," Annette remarks quickly.

"Exactly!" I nod. "I also suspect that her reaction is even more easily triggered because she has not been off leash for some time now. She needs to run, and we know that frustration intensifies behavior."

I have no doubt that Annette will be able to maintain any training I impart to Lexie. Therefore, I agree to keep her for several weeks.

In order to make absolutely sure that there is no misunderstanding between Lexie and me, I repeat, with positive motivation, all of the exercises she has learned so far. In the absence of any strong distraction, Lexie obeys and comes immediately and joyfully when called.

Now it's time to use the remote collar, as I have abandoned any hope for the efficacy of Thor's Chain. It is exceedingly rare that I have to use more than a medium level of intensity in a well-prepared dog, particularly a young and normally quite guidable one. Lexie, however, ignores the lower levels of intensity completely. At medium settings she gives a startled yip and jumps in the air—and keeps going! She continues to bolt after everything that draws her attention: running dogs, cats, squirrels, even cars. Only when I edge the intensity up does she finally respond. Over the course of the next few weeks, many reminders are necessary.

It is always a fascinating experience when the dog finally learns to control her own behavior without being forced or even prompted by the trainer. When Lexie detects a moving target, she visibly holds herself in check and waits for permission. Most of the time I allow her to meet the other dog or tree the squirrel, but for safety reasons she must pause until I release her. It is as if an impatient driver learns to stop at the red light before he resumes speed when it turns green.

Annette now takes Lexie on daily walks in the open space, to give her high energy a much-needed outlet.

"She is a joy at home, good with other dogs and children, and on walks it is wonderful to see how much fun she has running free. And yet, I feel completely in control," Annette tells me when Lexie comes to board at the kennel. "We finally have the dog we always wanted."

Life With
the Schnauzer Family
Life Without 'Father'

The Schnauzers with their "Daddy" Falko have spent exciting afternoon hours in the marshlands. Ammo particularly has developed a case of hero-worship for the German Shepherd Dog and follows him around like a pilot fish. Falko, unlike the Schnauzers, is not a natural rodent hunter. He had the unbelievable good fortune of a mouse practically jumping into his mouth. Now he peers intently and with a fatuous expression on his face into all the rodent holes in hopes another mouse might hop out.

The Schnauzers do not wait for such luck. They hunt as a pack. One digs at one end of the rodent warren and the other two locate the other entrances and begin digging from there. Sooner or later the mouse will make a break for freedom and one of Schnauzers gets an hors d'oeuvre. (I have never figured out if this teamwork is an inborn hunting skill or if they simply like to dig near each other.)

In the evening, after the dogs are fed, Falko goes out through the dog door and remains outside for about twenty minutes. This is nothing unusual. When he returns, however, and Ammo greets him like a long-lost relative, Falko growls at him. Ammo is upset and behaves even more deferentially. Since he is already taller than the German Shepherd Dog, instead of jumping up, he now bows down to lick Falko's mouth. Falko continues to growl and Ammo, not aware of any transgression on his part, is intensifying his appeasement behavior.

Something is wrong. Falko is normally exceedingly tolerant with his bearded charges. His abdomen is swollen and he is clearly agitated and in distress. Oh, good God! Bloat!

There is no time to lose. With shaking hands I call my vet's home number. Jim is at a fundraiser event, but his wife is trying to reach him there. Hurry, please.

Five minutes later Jim calls back. He is on his way and we are to meet him at his practice. By now Falko looks like he is going to explode; he is clearly in a lot of pain.

Jim, still in a tuxedo, inserts a needle right behind the ribcage into the stomach to release the accumulated gas. Next, a stomach tube is inserted and the stomach contents emptied. Falko endures all this with his usual amiable demeanor. The stomach still has to be untwisted. It would take some time to rouse assistance to perform such a complicated operation. It is now midnight. Once Falko is stabilized, we take off for the emergency clinic.

Falko is rushed into the operating room and I am pacing the floor, trying to hang on to some semblance of composure. Please, please, don't die.

Bloat. Gastric Torsion. Volvulus. What you call this hideous condition doesn't matter. That it is often lethal does. It is one of the horrors that large, deep-chested breeds often face. The stomach rotates on its long axis. Gas is trapped inside and blood supply to vital organs is practically clamped off. The onset is sudden and a painful death is imminent without immediate veterinary intervention. Dry kibble and overfeeding are often blamed as contributory causes. In Falko's case, however, they could not have played a part. He eats fresh food and is never overfed. Clearly, there is a strong genetic component to this terrible condition.

After an interminable time a vet appears. "I think he's going to be okay. He arrested once and we got him right back. If he arrests again—" she pauses.

"Is he going to have brain damage?" I ask. I am not sure what I am thinking.

"No, we got him right back, this time, but if—"

"If he arrests again, let him go," I manage to squeeze out between sobs. To hell with composure!

"He is stable now. With a little luck he'll make it," she says, giving me a flicker of hope.

But when the vet appears once more, I know.

"He arrested again and we weren't able to get him back. I'm sorry." There is compassion in her voice as she shakes her head.

It's not possible, I want to say. He is only nine. He is so healthy. He is such a happy dog. Just a few hours ago he was hunting with his family. He was so *alive*.

But I'm unable to speak, so I nod.

Falko is dead.

Every Day Is a
Good Judgment Day

Predatory behavior and aggression are undoubtedly the two most misunderstood traits in our domestic dogs. In my opinion, one cannot interact with dogs appropriately without a thorough understanding of both.

"She's gonna get the little kid!" the clueless observer is shouting. "Oh, God! I can't watch!"

Grendel, the large, powerful black German Shepherd bitch, is indeed bearing down at top speed on the curly-haired small boy, who has unwittingly trotted into her path of pursuit. Sapir, our protection-training helper, convincingly playing the "bad guy," had deliberately teased Grendel, then sped away to hide. With Sapir now concealed from Grendel's view, she targets the only moving creature in her sights: Sapir's three-year-old son Jonathan.

The spectators gasp in horror. Nevertheless, Betty, Grendel's owner, is making no attempt to call or stop her dog. Ten paces in front of Jonathan, Grendel veers almost imperceptibly and brushes past the tyke with undiminished momentum. Jonathan is dreamily unaware in his toddler world. It is as if a runaway truck has just barely sped past a blind and deaf person.

"Did you see that?" the spectators chatter to each other. "Unbelievable!"

Meanwhile, Grendel has cornered Sapir and barks at him forcefully. Betty approaches and calls her dog back.

161

"She found me too quickly. Let's do it again, and this time I'll try to make it harder for her to find me," Sapir huffs.

"Didn't you see what almost happened to your son?" the spectator, in a state of consternation, queries Sapir.

Sapir is a highly successful and experienced dog trainer. He shrugs and smiles indulgently. "Nothing almost happened. Jonathan often plays around here when we're working dogs. These dogs," he pats Grendel and points to my dog Ilka, "and dogs like them are perfectly clear in the head. Grendel was completely aware that she was pursuing me, not little Jonathan."

"But she appeared so *intent*," the spectator demurs, still a bit shaken.

Sapir is a patient man. "Predatory or hunting behavior is intense, but it is definitely *not* aggression directed toward prey. The motivations of the hunter are profoundly different from those of the fighter. Predatory behavior is part of the functional cycle of procuring nourishment," he explains. "It is *not* aggression," he repeats for emphasis.

"But what about those dogs who run after children and then bite or even mutilate them?" the spectator wants to know. "What about those Pit Bulls and other fighting dogs?"

"Listen," Sapir is on to one of his favorite subjects, "there are many unbalanced and disturbed dogs. They sense danger where there is none and they cannot discern between prey and an opponent; likewise, they are incapable of recognizing what is a game and what is not. Not all Pit Bulls are bad either. Those dogs that come from fighting strains, however, were selected for inherited aberrant social behavior as well as for excessive aggression and prey drive. They are not and can never be safely kept as pets, even if they are not trained to fight.

Every Day Is a Good Judgment Day

"It stands to reason," Sapir continues, "that it is completely abnormal for a social animal to attack so indiscriminately and viciously. If that were normal behavior, the species would have been extinct thousands of years ago. No training in the world could turn a normal, clearheaded dog like Grendel into a prize-winning fighting dog. Don't smear all dogs with the same brush."

Turning to Betty, who is standing next to Grendel, Sapir says, "Let's do it again. This time I'll hide in the bushes and let Grendel drag me out!"

Another spectator is trying to digest this new scenario. "You're not worried that she will bite you seriously?"

Sapir fought terrorists while he was in the Israeli Army; he is not scared of a game with a German Shepherd Dog. Now he answers mildly, "Not half as worried as you are, apparently."

Sapir speeds off while Betty is holding Grendel by the collar.

"Okay, send her!" comes Sapir's voice from the depth of the bushes.

Grendel shoots forward and, barking excitedly, circles the bush. When this fails to produce Sapir, she penetrates into the bush and, latching on to Sapir's burlap-covered leather sleeve, drags him out into the sunlight. Sapir praises her, slips out of the sleeve and lets her carry it around as her reward.

But Grendel is not ready to quit. This game is much too much fun. She parades around with the sleeve in her mouth and brings it back to Sapir, who obliges her by giving the sleeve a playful tug.

"Enough chasing me, enough of using her prey drive. I can't run anymore. Now let's see her defensive skills. I want to work with her aggression a bit," Sapir says loudly enough for the excitedly mumbling group of visitors to hear.

Barking Up the Right Tree

After having slipped back into his protective sleeve, not giving any warning, Sapir attacks, shouting loudly, his padded stick raised high above his head as if to strike. Sapir is nothing if not a good actor. I swear, if someone came at me in this manner, I'd still be running. Grendel, however, not backing up an inch, without hesitation and without fear, grips the sleeve and hangs on. When Sapir stands still, Grendel lets go reluctantly. She would rather continue the play-fight, but rules are rules and she has learned that violating the regulations ends the game. She is rewarded for her obedience by being allowed to carry the sleeve around and finally taking her booty back to the car.

"We'll work Ilka next," Sapir promises. "But first I better explain the process to our visitors," he adds with a conspiratorial twinkle in his eye.

"You can see, can't you, that Grendel felt in no way hostile toward me," Sapir begins, sitting down in the grass next to the spectators. "Why don't you bring Grendel back," he suggests to Betty, "so she can visit with us."

Grendel is a very self-confident and trusting soul and imbued with a general goodwill toward all people. She has never met a person she didn't consider a pal. Now she lands in Sapir's lap and even greets the spectators like friends.

"It really *is* just a game to her," one spectator observes, still a bit astounded, as reality crowds out the horror stories in his brain.

"Yes, it is a game that dogs take seriously—nothing more, nothing less. It is in a way like a martial-arts contest. The intensity is high, but both participants avoid hurting each other deliberately; the rules are understood and obeyed," Sapir explains.

"But—aggression, isn't aggression dangerous? You said you were working with her aggression, and—er—I mean—"

the spectator is babbling in his excitement.

"All mammals have aggression. They could not survive without it," Sapir explains. "Aggression can be very dangerous if it's fear-based. A self-assured dog is able to control his aggression very well; he's not likely to overreact out of insecurity."

"Like a fear-biter?" a spectator wants to know.

"Exactly," Sapir nods. "You can see there is no need for Grendel to be snappish or to threaten you. She's not afraid."

"I can see that now," another spectator admits.

"A clearheaded dog would never hurt anyone on purpose without a very good reason," Sapir continues, "And dogs who don't show good judgment and who aren't of stable temperament are not allowed to participate in this sport. They must undergo a fairly substantive temperament test first."

This is news to our spectators. "You mean, not just any old dog is allowed to compete in the sport of—what do you call it—Shits-hound?"

Sapir coughs. "Er—that's *Schutzhund*. It simply translates as protection dog, but it has evolved into an international dog sport, testing the dog's versatility in search work, obedience and agility and a stylized protection phase, like the one we just demonstrated."

"Amazing. I had no idea!" one spectator states the obvious.

"And what is most important," Sapir confides with a wide grin before he speeds off again, "is that it's a lot of fun for us and for the dogs!"

Betty has taken Grendel to the emergency veterinarian,

because she suspects that her dog has a foxtail deep in her ear. It is clearly painful; Grendel scratches at her ear and cries.

The vet, a young woman, peers at the black-and-brown bitch suspiciously. She evidently is afraid, perhaps because of previous bad experiences with German Shepherd Dogs.

"We have to take her into the back and snub her up tightly; I don't want to get bitten," she voices her fears.

"I don't think that's necessary," Betty demurs, "and in any case, I'm going to stay with my dog!"

Grendel gives no sign of fear or hostility, so the vet reluctantly agrees. "Okay, but hold her tightly! My face is going to be awfully close to her teeth."

She bends over Grendel and eases her otoscope into her ear. Grendel whimpers, but does not move.

"I can see a foxtail right on the eardrum," the vet reports, straightening up. "Your dog is very brave and didn't even flinch; she really is easy to work on," she adds, now stroking Grendel who is pleased with the attention. "If she holds this still I may be able to remove it without anaesthetizing her; the barbs are sticking up a bit."

Grendel endures the unpleasant procedure with her usual amiable compliance.

The young vet now reaches for the cookie jar to reward Grendel. "I wish all the dogs that come here were as easygoing as you," she coos to the bitch. "It's nice to have a German Shepherd Dog without aggression," she remarks to Betty by way of compliment.

Without thinking, Betty corrects her, "Actually, Grendel has a fair bit of aggression."

The veterinarian could not have looked more aghast if the jar of dog biscuits had transmogrified in her hands and grown poisonous fangs. Jumping away from Grendel she gasps, "She *does?*"

Every Day Is a Good Judgment Day

The emotional baggage many people attach to the mere mention of the word "aggression" is incomprehensible to me.

"She doesn't show *inappropriate* aggression," Betty tries to pour oil on the waves. "On the contrary, she's very trusting and friendly, as you could see for yourself."

"Yeah, she *is* very easy-going," the vet observes as Grendel pokes her with her nose, begging for more cookies. She kneels next to Grendel and feeds her several more treats, having evidently decided that Betty is a nutcase.

Life With
the Schnauzer Family
Strong, But Not So Silent

Betty and I are meeting friends for dinner at a nice restaurant. Ilka and Ammo are coming along for the ride. We
park my minivan right under a street light on a fairly busy
street and walk the short distance to our destination. It is a
cool night and the windows on the driver and passenger sides
are both open a few inches. As always, I leave the dogs with
the casual admonition to guard the car. This is just a recur-
ring little ritual that merely signals to the dogs that Vera will
be gone for a while. Of course, at the time I have no idea of
how literally my offhand request will be followed.

Our meal is rudely interrupted when a young man storms
into the restaurant, gesticulating wildly and announcing at
the top of his lungs, "There is a black Giant Schnauzer running around on the road!"

Betty and I gallop out onto the street and race the block
or so to my car in a panic. The windows were only cracked
and the doors were locked. Then how on Earth—? It couldn't
be Ilka or Ammo. Or could it? After all, how many
Riesenschnauzer are there in downtown San Rafael?

By the light of the street lamp as we approach, I can see
Ammo sitting in the driver's seat looking somewhat daunted.
Ilka is poking her head out the window above the side sliding door. *That* window doesn't even open! A woman is standing next to the minivan, petting Ilka. Good grief, is this lady

169

suicidal? There is broken glass everywhere on the sidewalk.

"What happened?" I gasp as I peer inside the car to reassure myself that the dogs are fine.

"I saw the whole thing," the woman informs us, now stepping away from Ilka and the shattered window. "A drunk was weaving by on the sidewalk, talking to himself rather loudly. Your dogs barked at him. This infuriated him so much that he kicked your car and drummed with both fists on the roof, shouting obscenities at the dogs. I guess the jerk felt courageous, because the windows were closed," she reports with a scornful curl of her lips. This dog," she points at Ilka, "broke through the window and jumped at him."

My mouth is dry and Betty stares disbelievingly. "Did she bite him?" I am looking for blood among all the glass. There is none.

"No," the woman grins, "but she plowed him right against the wall of a house and held him there for a long time. That man didn't know what hit him. He absolutely froze."

"And then?" I still can hardly believe my ears.

"Then, after a minute or so, she simply turned around and hopped back into the car. That guy didn't dare to move for at least another minute. So I stood by her to keep her in the car until you arrived."

"What about the other one?" I inquire about Ammo.

"I think he was a little afraid when your bitch broke out the window. He hasn't made a sound since," the woman reports.

My little hero!

"He's big, but he's really only eight months old." I am babbling, probably to relieve my anxiety while my brain is still desperately trying to catch up. "But how did you know where we were? There are at least ten restaurants within a block!"

170

Strong, But Not So Silent

"Oh, I just grabbed someone off the sidewalk and sent him into *all* the restaurants to announce that a black Giant Schnauzer was loose," this remarkable woman tells us.

One simply has to admire her presence of mind and be grateful for her good dog-sense.

"But weren't you afraid that she might attack *you* after the little episode you had just witnessed?"

The woman looks at me as if I'm an imbecile. "She's a perfectly reasonable dog. I knew I had nothing to fear from her." She cuts short our verbose expressions of gratitude, "Go, before someone calls the police."

"But we've done nothing wrong. Ilka didn't even bite," I demur rather daftly.

"Go! Get out of here!" the woman insists, and of course she is right.

Schutzhund training is over and all the cognoscenti engage in their customary after-training shoptalk. This is even better accomplished when lubricated by generous amounts of beer. Ilka is lying in the shade of a tree, taking a well-deserved nap. Our training helper's three-year-old daughter Ashley is in the process of securing Ilka as a play partner. Ashley is fearless.

She trots up to the bitch and shouts in her ear, "Ilka wake up!"

Ilka has no intention of interrupting her nap, but Ashley is determined as only a toddler can be. She grabs Ilka by her beard with both little fists and pulls with all her might. Ilka would *never* tolerate this impudence from an adult stranger. Poor fool who tried it! But she knows the difference, and so she gets to her feet.

The little girl now leads her around by her beard, much as one would lead a horse by the halter, singing, "Ilka-Pilka, Ilka-Pilka." Ilka follows her demurely, clearly recognizing this as a game and giving the human puppy a great deal of latitude.

Ilka, like the other dogs, has just gone through a training sequence that included holding a man immobile by barking at him, running after him and biting him when he escapes, as well as fending off a strong attack. Yet no one fears for Ashley's safety, least of all I. Most, if not all, Schutzhund-trained dogs that day would have acted similarly, precisely for the reason that they had been selectively bred for a high degree of confidence.

Aggression is probably the most misunderstood trait in our domestic dogs. Uninformed people think any kind of aggression is dangerous. The muddleheaded attempts of many pet and show-dog breeders to water down all species-specific behavior through selective breeding result in vast numbers of meek, not infrequently fearful dogs. This fear then turns into unsure aggression under certain circumstances. The analogy of a nervous, timid person packing a gun with a hair trigger comes to mind. Whereas a skittish dog is likely to growl or snap at the slightest perceived threat, a dog who is *confident* is actually very unlikely to damage anyone, because he bites only as a last resort when other means to get his point across have failed. Just as with humans, it is the coward one must fear, not the brave person.

The debate about whether or to what degree fear and aggression are inherited or acquired traits rages on between behaviorists and ethologists. I believe, along with most ethologists, that there is compelling evidence that, although environmental factors have an impact, fear and aggression are strongly influenced by genetic factors. If only stable dogs with emotional resilience were bred, the index of dog bites would be reduced drastically.

Although most of my dogs, past and present, were and are endowed with a great deal of confident aggression, all my veterinarians appreciate how easy it is for them to work on them: not much fear, particularly not of people, therefore no inappropriate aggression. I use my dogs for demonstrations in elementary schools, an event that the dogs enjoy almost as much as the children.

The Princess
is a Trifle Timid

Fear and unsure defensive aggression are flip sides of the same coin. In some cases I am able to activate and develop other strong inborn behaviors to counter-condition and desensitize the fearful dog.

The young black-and-white Border Collie shrieks in fear as her owner pulls her through the door to my office. You would think she was being led to her slaughter. The slightest movement on my part sends her scurrying to the end of her leash.

"Tinkerbell is a little fearful," her owner remarks, to no one in particular, a film of honey coating his voice.

A little fearful, my foot!

Gary is a slightly portly middle-aged man with a distracted, irresolute demeanor. "She's shy with people she doesn't know," he says mildly to the room.

A delicate clarification of the facts seems in order. "She isn't a little shy; she's bloody terrified."

"Well—" Gary finally looks at me, dismay in his eyes. "She's really a sweet dog. I just think she needs a bit of training."

A bit of training, indeed! The way it looks, a lobotomy is more like it. It is very difficult to work with owners who are willfully oblivious to their dogs' shortcomings.

While I am still pondering how to crack the shell of Gary's denial, he interrupts my ruminations.

Barking Up the Right Tree

"Tinkerbell does come around, once she knows you."

"Oh yeah? And how long does that usually take?" I ask him.

"Oh, not that long," says Gary vaguely. "Usually a few weeks. She's still a little afraid of my brother, although she's getting better."

"Gary, that statement doesn't give me any useful information. How often does your brother come to visit you?"

"He's staying with us for a few weeks. Now Tinkerbell only barks at him when he stands up. As long as he's sitting down she's okay."

Oh, surely, *that* is progress. Maybe they can glue the wretched brother to a chair. "Has she always been this way?" I ask, looking at the quivering heap of misery hiding behind Gary's chair.

"Well, she's only ten months old. When my wife and I picked her up from the breeder, she was the most reserved one in the litter. That's why we liked her." He smiles dreamily with the certitude that he has made an auspicious choice.

"That was — er — uninformed," I shake my head. "Many people make the mistake of choosing the most pathetic puppy in the litter, because they want a laid-back dog later on. Bad decision. You are on much safer ground selecting the friendliest, most outgoing one. Were you able to see the mother? I bet she was just like Tinkerbell!"

"We weren't allowed to see the mother," Gary recalls. "The breeder told us she would be upset by strangers, because she has puppies. We could hear her barking behind a door, though," Gary says righteously, as if concealing the pup's crazy mother from prospective buyers were somehow justifiable. "And," Gary says with as much emphasis as he can marshal, "the pups are AKC registered!"

I have to swallow hard to avoid frothing at the mouth.

The Princess is a Trifle Timid

There's a special place in hell for breeders like that, I mutter, not for the first time, to myself. Aloud I say, "Gary, Gary. Don't you realize that nothing, absolutely nothing, precludes a litter from being registered with the American Kennel Club, as long as both parents are of the same breed? There is not a *single disqualifying fault* that prevents so-called purebred dogs from being mated and their litters AKC registered. The parent animals could be insane, afflicted with a host of hereditary diseases, vicious, ugly, oversize, undersize, toothless, blind, deaf, and so on.

"The AKC is merely a registry of numbers; it is *not* a guarantee of quality. The AKC leaves *all* the accountability up to the individual breeder. And breeders come in all varieties: A few are knowledgeable, honest and critical about their breeding program; most are either ignorant or greedy or both."

"Well, anyway, she was the sweetest in the litter," Gary contends and, turning to his shivering dog, he coos, "We love her and—don't we my little sweetie-pie, she's our little pumpkin, she's daddy's darling, and mummy loves her too— "

Such a heartwarming and tender moment in the life of owner and dog! I'm glad I haven't had breakfast yet.

Gary finally interrupts his infantile gurgling as he glimpses me staring at the ceiling and tapping my foot. "I want to see if there is anything that can be done to bring her out of it."

"Gary, that isn't going to be trivial, if it can be done at all. Her propensity to react fearfully is inherited and will always be present to some degree. I hope we can give her sufficiently pleasant experiences to alleviate her fright. If we don't, her fear will turn to full-fledged fearful aggression as she gets older. And you exacerbate her problem by—"

"We took her to puppy class," Gary goes on like a wind-

177

up toy, "but she was completely miserable; she wouldn't even play with the other puppies. Then we had a trainer come to the house, because Tinkerbell has such a hard time away from home."

"What did you do with her in those lessons?" I ask.

"We taught her to sit and walk on a leash. She never learned to lie down on command. The trainer said to socialize her more," Gary tells me. "He also said Tinkerbell is a very sweet and non-aggressive dog," he adds defensively. "But my vet recommended that I take her to you," he explains with a frown, as if he doubted his vet's sanity.

"Have you done any systematic socialization with her?" I inquire, ignoring his tone.

"Well, we take her to the dog park several times a week. She's now all right with other dogs, but she is terrified of people, except me and my wife."

"So she isn't properly socialized at all," I say. Socializing means to teach the dog to show appropriate behavior in a variety of social settings: with other dogs, with people, with children, at the vet's, and so on. Merely exposing her hasn't made much of a difference, it seems. Simply doing more of a technique that is not working in the first place does not improve your chances of succeeding. Exposure alone either shows substantial improvement very rapidly, like in a week or two, or it is not going to bring about any significant positive change."

"You don't sound very encouraging," Gary complains.

"I'm not, that's correct. I'm not even sure we can effect any crucial change in the long run."

"What do you mean by in the long run?"

"If we work long enough in the same place and under the same circumstances, we *will* improve her behavior. However, there is no guarantee that she will maintain that behavior under even slightly different conditions," I elaborate. "And furthermore, you make the problem worse by dealing with her as if she were an imbecile, incapable of functioning normally. If you treat an emotionally fragile dog like a weak dog, his problem will become worse."

Gary runs a chubby hand through his sparse hair. "What do you mean?"

"You must manage an overly sensitive or shy dog as if he were a strong dog in order to help him overcome some of his weakness," I paraphrase.

Gary smiles blandly.

"It's a Zen kind of thing," I say breezily.

Gary gives me a bewildered look.

Well, I'm here to teach, so I make one more attempt, "You're not helping her when you pamper her like the princess on the pea."

"She also doesn't listen very well, especially when there are people around." Gary has hardly heard a word I said.

"Gary, even if you had trained her correctly, which I suspect you have not, she *cannot* obey if she's in a panic mood."

Like many of my clients, at least at the beginning, Gary has an exceedingly simplistic idea of dog training and a good portion of unwillingness to acknowledge how deep-seated his dog's aberrant behavior really is.

On my training field I offer Tinkerbell treats. She is much too inhibited to approach me, but she does pick up the food when I throw it in her direction, about six feet away. Since she is already thin, it would be absurd to try to increase her desire for food by putting her on a weight-loss diet.

"We've tried to have people feed her at the dog park, but she's afraid to come close to anyone," Gary tells me.

"I'm not really surprised. A dog who is in profound emotional distress doesn't want food; he wants security. And security in Tinkerbell's case means distance."

"There is nothing you can do?" Gary asks dolefully.

"I'm not through yet. There is one more thing I want to try," I say, fetching the Puppy Fishing toy.

Tinkerbell's interest is piqued instantly as she sees the toy fly through the air and scurry along the ground, past her nose. Giving me a sideways glance and assuring herself that I am far enough away, more than ten feet, she gives pursuit to the fluffy critter on the rope.

Glory Hallelujah! The dog has strong prey behavior! I give Tinkerbell a couple of easy successes and let her latch on to the toy. She holds it, but as soon as her attention slips I yank it away. The longer we play, the more skillful she gets and the more intent she becomes on the toy.

"What's this supposed to do?" Gary is becoming impatient. He probably thinks that he does not need to spend money on having me play with his dog.

But I have no time for him now and wave at him dismissively. "I'll explain later!" I shout to him.

When Tinkerbell hears me raise my voice, she stops and looks around fearfully. Damnation!

But quickly she shifts her attention back to the toy flying past her nose. We play until she begins to get tired. When she catches the toy she throws herself to the ground and gnaws at it. Now I approach a few steps. The young Border Collie gets up and takes her toy with her. She is not fatigued enough yet. Deliberately but carefully, I work her beyond her physical condition. Each time she has caught the toy and lies down with it for a respite, I approach, holding the toy on the string by the whip handle. She can leave, but she must also leave her toy. And, due to her fatigue, skittering

(Recalculated)

away becomes more and more of an effort.

Finally, I can stand next to her, and the following time she lets me touch her.

I give her a break and leave her gnawing on her toy.

"If I hadn't seen this with my own eyes I wouldn't have believed it," Gary says slowly, his resistance melting. "I have never seen anyone she didn't know very well approach her the way you did. I could try this at the dog park and get someone to pet her—"

"Oh no, you don't!" I shoot back. "This is our last chance. The slightest mistake now and we could lose the war. Play with her at home, in your yard. She needs to become even more possessive of the Puppy Fishing toy. She must become so monomaniacal about it that she would go through a brick wall to get it and *keep* it."

"You make her so tired that she can't run away, and that way people can touch her and she recognizes they mean no harm," he sums up his observation, showing a smidgen of alacrity at last.

"No, Gary, the process is more complex. There are many elements working in concert. It is true that a fatigued animal will change behavior to economize strength. But there is more to it than that. The better Tinkerbell gets at catching the prey-toy, the harder I make it for her to succeed, because frustration builds desire. We know that strong desire breaks down inhibitions. For instance, when a wild animal is very hungry, it will brave human presence and steal food. This newly found confidence will bring about success and a certain decrease of fear will remain with the animal. There is good reason why wild animals who have attacked humans or dogs near a residence are relocated or killed."

"Sounds complicated," says Gary, "but I can see that it is working."

Barking Up the Right Tree

Of course, I cannot resist the urge to spread enlightenment. I would like to make *every* owner or trainer an expert on dog behavior. (But I am not deluding myself that this can actually be accomplished.)

"I am grossly simplifying the process in the first place, and that's by far not all of it," I continue. "When a predator strikes prey, or in this case a prey substitute, it results in a release of tension. A dog who carries a toy calmly and proudly is mostly in a state of inner peace. In addition, prolonged physical activity lowers anxiety."

"I see," says Gary with a vacuous expression.

It's a lost cause. Well, if Gary follows my instructions, we will be able to help the young Border Collie, even if he doesn't understand why it is working.

Gary has done his homework. Already in the parking lot, Tinkerbell cavorts impatiently while he is getting the Puppy Fishing toy out of his station wagon. On the way to the training field, she leaps for it eagerly, having eyes for nothing else. There is no sign of the quivering mass of jelly she was the last time I saw her.

"She's fanatical about this toy," Gary reports. "I have to hide it from her, but she knows every hiding place and just sits in front of the closet we keep it in. When we play, it's hard to take the toy away from her; she won't let go."

"Great. Good work, Gary. Let me play with her and see for myself."

When Tinkerbell is chasing the toy she is completely focused. A bomb could fall in the neighbor's yard and she wouldn't hear it. When she catches the toy, I relax the string without approaching her. She stands holding the fluffy thing fully in her mouth, and her eyes glaze over under half-closed lids. It is almost as if she were going into a trance. Beautiful!

The Princess is a Trifle Timid

A canine who has hunted and killed a rabbit often stands or lies in a trance, holding his prey. Being an avid watcher of nature specials on television, I have noticed that this trance after the kill is also in the behavioral repertoire of big cats like lions and cheetahs.

It takes the young Border Collie a long time to release the toy and come back into the real world. When she does, the prey-toy on its string comes alive again.

In the next round, in a dance of gradual give-and-take, of tightening and releasing, slowly, hand over hand, I work myself closer until I can stroke Tinkerbell while she is standing with the toy in her mouth. She makes no attempt to retreat.

Now I continue by letting her catch the prey-toy on my body, first while I am lying down, and a bit later she has to jump at me to get it. She does so with only the slightest hesitation at first.

"She looks like a totally different dog," Gary says, when I give Tinkerbell, or rather myself, a break. Tinkerbell would keep on playing.

"Do you play ball and tug games with her at home?" I ask him.

"Oh yes! She loves playing ball and we play tug games with towels."

"Well, she has a lot of inborn prey behavior, but that withers if it isn't kept alive. The fact that you do will probably make all the difference between being able to train her successfully, as opposed to her becoming a walking panic button."

"You mean it's good?"

"Yes, Gary, it's very good!"

Now that Tinkerbell has overcome her fear of me, we go on with the first phase of the Rocket Recall. I hold the dog by the collar and Gary runs away, his pockets full of treats. When the young Border Collie arrives, she is allowed to jump at Gary for her food. As secondary reward follows a brief tug game with a fluffy squeaky-toy on a string. Tinkerbell is having a lot of fun and she has visibly opened up. I send Gary home to continue working with the toy and also to concentrate on the Rocket Recall with food.

Gary reports that he practiced the Rocket Recall with his wife holding Tinkerbell and that the dog really enjoyed the exercise.

The next project consists of having a stranger play Puppy Fishing with her. We need to see if her newfound confidence maintains. My training partner Betty is the guinea pig. When she enters the training field, the Border Collie scurries backwards, wuffing all the way. But as soon as Betty picks up the toy, Tinkerbell forgets all about her fear and chases it with abandon. Very soon Betty can stroke her while the dog is holding her toy. The young Border Collie's addled puppy brain is making the connection: When I hold a toy it feels good, and I am safe!

To my elation and surprise, Betty is now able to take Tinkerbell's training to another level of accomplishment. Betty always carries treats in her pockets and when Tinkerbell drops her toy, she offers her some tasty morsels. Without hesitation, the dog takes them from her hand and looks for more. The young Border Collie now almost boldly pushes for food, and Betty walks backward slowly, feeding her all the while. Another new association is forming in Tinkerbell's muddled little brain: Treats are good, treats are *safe*!

But why didn't that work before? A suspicion creeps into my brain and like the clunky detective in a whodunit who finally stumbles onto the solution, I feel like slapping my forehead and saying, *Mon Dieu, quelle imbecile! Ze solution, it was zere, before my very eyes.*

I had attributed all the young Border Collie's behavior to her excessive fear. In the process I failed to ascertain exactly what kind of attempts at training had been made. Gary had used treats to trick Tinkerbell into coming. Once she fell for it, she was snatched and put on leash or placed outside, etc. This stopped working very soon, because no animal is thick-witted enough to walk into a trap once they recognize it as such. (If dogs were that stupid, their species would have gone the way of the saber-toothed tiger long ago.) Confronted with these exceedingly clumsy and ineffective methods, the dog learns to distrust all the gestures that are ordinarily designed to demonstrate the trainer's good intentions. Treats, bending or crouching down, coaxing, all become mere precursors to something unpleasant.

With the new regimen of getting many treats without having to suffer unpleasant consequences, Tinkerbell's confidence is noticeably improving. She now takes food from me without hesitation.

I need another stranger. Fortuitously, a friend from Search and Rescue training, herself an accomplished dog trainer, has stopped by. Immediately, I recruit her to play Puppy Fishing with the Border Collie, who engages in the game without hesitation. After only a short while my friend is able to coax Tinkerbell to her and feed her when she arrives.

We are on a roll! I am fairly sanguine about the outcome of Tinkerbell's training now. Luckily, Gary has never used a toy to trick her. This fact, together with her exceedingly strong and well-developed prey-play behavior, gave us a foot in the door. And once the door was open, we could get in and build a system of positive *safe* signals.

Barking Up the Right Tree

Next, Gary has to take Tinkerbell back to the dog park and have all kinds of people feed her.

"When she is leery of someone, give him or her a handful of food and ask that person to feed her," I instruct him. "*Now* it will work, I think. Let her view strangers as walking vending machines; this makes her feel safe. But under no circumstances are these people to reprimand her for jumping or being unruly," I caution him. "The last thing we need now is to punish her confidence."

He assures me that he knows people who would cooperate.

"And, Gary," I endeavor to make my point once more, "resist the urge to baby her so much. You're not doing her any favors by cooing to her in a sugary voice. Praise her when she shows *confidence*, not when she displays uncertainty!"

In our next session, Gary reports that Tinkerbell is hitting everybody up for food. "That's good, isn't it?"

"Yes, Gary, it's good. She needs to see people as potential food sources. It makes her feel secure. In a few months you can stop pushing food into everybody's hand, but for now, you need to keep on."

In training, we proceed fairly uneventfully to the Sit and Down with food and toy motivation. Tinkerbell's confidence continues to improve beyond what I thought possible at the beginning. There is usually still a split-second hesitation when she meets a new person or encounters a new situation. This, in all probability, will never change. Nevertheless, she has become a relatively well-adjusted young dog.

See Lady Run

There is a strong inherited component to aggressive and fear behaviors. To some extent, these behaviors can be increased or diminished by the appropriate experiences. Excessive fear or aggression, however, cannot be successfully and lastingly ameliorated.

"Lady was abused when she was young," Jill informs me.

The medium-sized brown dog of indefinite heritage sits shaking by her owner's chair. She is drooling and there are moist footprints all over the tile floor in my office. If she were a human she would be nervously perspiring, but being a canine, only her feet sweat. The slightest movement or sound intensifies her quaking and salivating.

"How old is Lady and how long have you had her?"

"She's three years or thereabouts. We've had her for over two years. When we adopted her, we were told she was a stray and had been abused. That's why we took her. We felt so sorry for her. But now she's snapping at our grandchild. We tried to take her to training classes, but she just sat there and shivered."

I can imagine the answer, but I ask anyway. "How do you know she was abused?"

"Well—" Jill rummages through her purse and produces a sheet of paper and hands it to me. "This is the evaluation we got from the rescue organization when we adopted Lady."

According to the rescue organization's record, Lady had indeed been a stray and had been trapped by a romantic, kindhearted soul and delivered to the adoption agency.

The equally kind and romantic people at the agency assiduously "evaluated" Lady and filled out a piece of paper attesting to her adoptability and good character.

Housebroken: Yes

Aggressive: No

Socialized: Yes

Temperament: Friendly

Special observation: Was abused.

Et cetera.

May the Patron Saint of Dogs deliver us from the incompetence and clairvoyance of wide-eyed rescuers, I want to say, but I control my impulse and ask, "What have you done to work around her fear behavior?"

"Well, the adoption agency told us all she needed was love and socialization, because she's an abused dog. But we've have tried to socialize and expose her to various environments for months. It was torture for her. She's terrified of everything—people, cars, and noises. We can't let her off the leash at all. If anything frightens her, she panics and just keeps running. When we have her on the leash she drags us all the way back to the house. She hates riding in the car; she always gets sick. The only time she seems relaxed is at home. And even there, when the phone rings, she crawls under the sofa. But she's very sweet."

"She's been reacting like this to the phone for two years?"

"Yes, from the time we got her," Jill says.

Just being in my office is clearly extremely stressful for Lady. She is lying down as if she were going to sleep, with a glazed look in her eyes. Her body is shivering convulsively. If she were a computer, one would speak of system shutdown due to overload.

"Does she play with balls or tug toys at home?" I ask.

"No, not really," is the answer I expected.

Not surprisingly, Lady is not a good eater, although she is quite thin.

"Jill, there is nothing I can do to help you. There are now psychoactive drugs being prescribed for dogs, but in my experience they only sedate them. The dogs I have seen on drug therapy have been zombies, but you might explore the option with your vet. I recommend that you categorically separate Lady and your grandson. I have seen many cases like this and my prognosis is that Lady will remain dysfunctional, except at home without any other people present. I am sorry."

"I don't really want to start with drugs," Jill shakes her head.

"I think it best to keep her at home where she is at least reasonably happy." This is the best advice I can give under the circumstances.

"You don't think we have made her problem worse, do you? Even at home she is not really a happy dog."

"Jill, I don't hesitate to hold the owner responsible when it is called for, but none of Lady's disturbed behavior is your fault."

"What should we be looking for if we ever adopted another dog?" Jill wants to know.

"Get the most confident, friendly one you can find. Don't be dissuaded if the dog is a little boisterous and unruly; that can be controlled through training. But no training in the world is going to materially change an emotionally unsound, nervous or phobic dog."

It is time for one of my soapboxes again.

Countless times I have heard similar stories from disappointed and disillusioned owners. I am appalled at rescue organizations that con people into taking their mentally ill dogs by inventing stories of alleged abuse. A lot of love, a little socialization, a bit of training and everything is going to be fine. If rescue organizations classified these dogs as profoundly behaviorally or mentally disturbed, no one would adopt them. It is evidently more productive to evoke sympathy and guilt than to call it like it is.

To be sure, there are abused dogs. But if a dog is essentially sound, we *do* know that he is able to change his behavior fairly rapidly once his circumstances improve. Many of these purportedly abused dogs have inherited deep-seated aberrant behavior and are never going to change in any significant way. To distinguish between inherited or acquired aberrations (and the interaction between the two factors) without knowledge of the dog's history is nearly impossible in the short term, even for experts. Careful observation and evaluation over several weeks, sometimes months, as well as knowledge of the dog's parentage, are necessary.

If there were as many homes as there are unwanted dogs, one *might* make an argument that all should be saved. However, tragically, but undeniably, many more dogs are seeking homes than are available. Some dogs will be sacrificed so others can be saved. It seems only judicious and rational to me that we should rescue the mentally and emotionally healthy ones who enjoy their lives and are able to fit easily into most owners' homes.

Life With the Schnauzer Family
Rules Are Rules

The Schnauzer twins are now nine months old and both are taller than their mother. They haven't filled out yet and Ammo especially looks like a big black cardboard cutout. Already he weighs almost ninety pounds. When he stands on his hind legs he can put his feet comfortably over my shoulders. I am five-foot-eight.

The Schnauzerkinder and I sorely miss Falko. This shift in the social structure makes Ammo halfheartedly try to improve his ranking. All the older female dogs outrank him; there is no chance to unseat them. The squabbles with his sister always end in a draw. Gandhi and Ben are too old to be taken seriously. But maybe he could nibble away at Vera's authority. This, of course, as I could have told him, is an utterly fatuous little notion.

I have brought home giant shank bones from the butcher, one for each dog. For the Schnauzer twins it is their first experience with so delicious a treat. For a while I hear contented gnawing from all corners of the deck and yard. I have always been able to take even the most appetizing morsels away from my dogs. Although *I exercise this option very sparingly*, I take comfort in the knowledge that I could remove poisonous or dangerous items from their jaws without losing a finger. The Schnauzerkinder have yet to learn this. When I approach Apache and reach for the bone, she is not pleased, but on my insistence she lets go reluctantly. Immediately, I return her prize and praise her. Ammo, however, growls menacingly when I come near. This fledgling social aggression is undesirable, but not yet dangerous behavior. It is tantamount to the comment, Bugger off and let me eat! When I ostentatiously reach for the bone, his growling intensifies and his paws clamp on to his cherished possession. This is unacceptable. I take my fist and rap my knuckles on top of his head, shouting, "Cut that out, you little twerp!" Ammo is so shocked that his otherwise so lenient owner is growling back at him that he relinquishes his bone without another peep. Naturally, he gets his bone back, and that is that.

But Ammo wants to try one more time to climb the ladder to the command post. I am reading in bed and Ammo is reclining at the foot of the bed. He *loathes* being disturbed when he is resting. This always puts him in an exceedingly disagreeable frame of mind. As my foot inadvertently touches him, he roars his disapproval. It is my bed and I move my foot wherever and whenever I want! He can go take his indignation and roar somewhere else! I pull my knees up to my chin and with both feet catapult Ammo out of the bed, roaring back at him. From then on, whenever his eminence Ammo feels himself incommoded when on my bed, he grumbles and leaves precipitately.

Never again does he challenge my leadership.

Sooner or later, many, if not most, dogs will make more or less benign attempts to assert their superiority. This is normal behavior and no reason for the dog owner to become frightened or worse, hysterical. If the owner is sure in his or her role as compassionate leader, s/he will intuitively react appropriately.

Rules Are Rules

Recognizing incipient social aggression is of the utmost importance, as is dealing with the situation quickly and decisively. It is not funny when your dog growls at you when he is on the bed, as some foolish owners seem to think. Nor is it funny when a dog throws a fit when he is being bathed or having his nails clipped. However, *overreacting* is every bit as inappropriate as underreacting and may escalate the situation needlessly. If the dog is being raised from a puppy, a capable pack leader has to resort to harshness only very occasionally.

My dominance over the Schnauzer Family is not established primarily by a show of physical prowess. I raise my dogs in a very lenient environment, yet I do not—*ever*—accept their occasional I will not! If I meet opposition, usually I break even simple requirements down into smaller fractions that the dog can accomplish easily, rewarding each step, but he *must* at least try to cooperate.

Many conditions can trigger the dog's attempt to establish his dominance. Age and hormones are the most common reasons. Some breeds and individuals are from the beginning more likely to challenge their owners than others. Likewise, any changes in the dog's social structure, the family-pack, often set the scene for a canine putsch.

The Terror
of the Neighborhood

Unsure defensive, fearful aggression can, of course, also be directed toward other dogs.

Sally, the petite, slender, middle-aged lady in my office, looks as if she collided with an eighteen-wheeler. Her face shines in all rainbow colors and is covered with scabs of crusted blood, as are her hands. Her black Belgian Sheepdog, Puck, is lying by her side, doing his best to appear angelic and well-behaved. He seems like a friendly, well-adjusted animal and it never occurs to me that he could be the source of these lacerations.

"As you can see," Sally raises her hands to her face, "I really need your help."

I am speechless, which is not a state in which I find myself very often. If Sally's dog did *this* to her and she wants to keep him anyway, she needs an ambitious psychiatrist, not a dog trainer. But then, the injuries really look nothing like dog bites.

"Puck is a dog fighter, and—"

"And you got in the middle of a dog fight? Not a good idea!" I cut in keenly.

"I know *that*," Sally moves a weary hand. "Puck was going after another dog, a smaller one, and I knew if I let go of the leash, he'd kill it. So I was hanging on while Puck dragged me along the gravel and through several bushes. This was the fifth time something like that happened. The injuries from the last time hadn't even healed. My doctor finally recommended I get rid of my dog before I got seriously hurt."

I infer that "getting rid of" translates as euthanasia.

"How old is Puck, and for how long has this been going on?" I need to know.

Puck is four years old, in his prime. He was castrated before he was a year old. As a youngster, Puck was not antagonistic toward other dogs, although on many occasions he was not completely at ease with them. Sometimes he would run away or cower. After the age of two, when he was mature, he began to be gradually more belligerent with other dogs, not discriminating between males and females. By the age of three he had been in several minor scuffles without serious injuries to either dog. Progressively, the fights became more serious, often resulting in injuries to the combatants. As a result of his proclivities, Puck had not been allowed off the leash for over a year. Sally had taken him through several obedience courses.

Sally looks at me apprehensively. "Can you help me?"

"It all depends," I say taking a deep breath and shaking my head, "if he *can't* or *won't* control himself under these conditions. In some dogs the anxiety shoots up so high that the point of no return is reached almost instantly. Pressure from the outside only aggravates the situation. If, however, he can control himself, then we can do it from the outside."

"He was neutered when he was still very young," Sally says, "but it doesn't seem to have made any difference."

"That's not necessarily true," I reply. "Let me explain. There are two types of aggression. Type one is active aggression, sometimes referred to as 'dominance' or 'social' aggression. It is expressed mainly in *competitive* situations, usually against other male dogs, although occasionally it extends to humans. Castration, especially if done early enough, can sometimes ameliorate this type of behavior. And what is more important, a castrated male does not usually *draw* aggression from other male dogs. Type two is reactive, or defensive, aggression, usually triggered by wariness or fear. Castration does nothing to alleviate this. In an uncastrated male, you might have had a synergy of the two types of aggression. We'll never know."

Sally is a quick student. "So you think Puck's behavior is fear induced?"

"I think so. The fact that he does not distinguish between male and female dogs supports my hypothesis."

"But why on Earth does he not distinguish between small and large dogs? He can't be afraid of the little ones," Sally asks.

"He has become a bully. It's now a case of *I'll get you before you get me, and I know I can!* The coward's courage."

"You hear that?" Sally says to Puck who is the picture of suave elegance and looks like butter wouldn't melt in his mouth.

"It's a no-win situation. If another dog beats him, he is going to be more afraid and try harder the next time. If he prevails, his confidence in his own ability to beat his opponent increases," I explain.

"When he was young he was so submissive and uneasy around other dogs, he usually tried to avoid them. I never thought he would become aggressive," she tells me, shaking her head.

A variation of this pronouncement I have heard hundreds of times. It always denotes a deep lack of understanding of the nature of aggression.

"You see avoidance, uneasiness; I see defensive aggression," I tell her.

"I don't understand." Sally shakes her head, frowning.

"Defensive behavior and evasive behavior are flip sides of the same coin," I clarify. "They have the same purpose—namely, to avert or neutralize a threat."

"That makes sense." Sally is catching on fast. "But I still don't understand when —"

"Whether the animal is going to react with fight or flight depends on all kinds of different factors," I anticipate her question. "Age, prior experiences, location. If it cannot flee, for instance, it will fight. Animals are more likely to fight on territory with which they are familiar or near someone from whom they expect support. That is one reason why dogs have a greater propensity for aggression on the leash. They cannot evade because they are tethered, and their confidence is boosted because Daddy or Mommy is right behind them."

"Puck will fight even when he is not on leash and by himself," Sally says bitterly. "When there are no other dogs around he is very obedient."

This, of course, I have to see to believe. What *owners* consider obedience and what *I* consider obedience are often two completely different things. Glancing at Puck, I cannot really imagine him displaying this thoroughly aberrant behavior. In my many years of training dogs and their owners, however, I have learned to trust my feelings in regard to both. Sally is no fool. She may be petite, but her demeanor is resolute and her interaction with her dog is loving and firm.

"What have you done to alleviate the problem?" I ask her.

"Well, first I worked with obedience. He will usually ignore another dog when he is on a Down-Stay. That is, unless the other dog is off-leash and approaches him. In that case he tries to kill that dog. I've jerked him as hard as I could on a pinch collar. I'm pretty strong, but it seems to make him even more frantic. Then I've worked with desensitization and counter-conditioning. You know, worked around other dogs and tried to get him to pay attention to food or a toy. That was singularly unsuccessful," Sally says, hanging her head.

"It would be. Desensitization in particular is probably the least successful training technique in any but the most superficial cases. And in counter-conditioning the new focus has to produce more intensity of feeling than the original one. In Puck's case I cannot imagine what that could be."

"So you can't help me?" Sally looks despondent. "That's bad news. You're my last hope. I called my vet to ask him if tranquilizers would work, but he told me it would only make Puck attack a little more slowly. He suggested I call you. Believe me, I've tried everything else."

A scary choice. Achieve success or it is curtains for Puck. "I don't know yet, Sally, if and how I can help you. I need a little more information."

On my training field, Sally demonstrates Puck's obedience. To my considerable surprise, he is attentive and responds immediately to her commands, even under various distractions. However, when Sally takes him near another dog whom I have prudently deposited behind an impenetrable wire fence, Puck's demeanor changes drastically. He hurls himself at the fence with all his might, bared teeth first, growling and barking in a hoarse guttural voice. Even when Sally drops the leash and runs in the opposite direction, Puck keeps up his fearsome show.

I am, of course, aware that the relative security of the fence, as well as the frustration of fighting against a barrier, make dogs appear bolder than they really are. However, if Puck shows even a fraction of the same aggression when he meets another dog on his walk, it has to be quite an impressive and frightening display.

Barking Up the Right Tree

Back in my office, Puck is in a sociable mood, bringing toys and wanting to be petted as if the whole nasty incident had never happened.

I would like to help, but the situation puts me in a considerable quandary. I am now quite certain that Puck is able to control his behavior based on the rest of his demeanor. He is not a nervous, timid dog. If Puck were mine, I am confident that I could regulate his behavior in a short time. (If he were mine the problem would never have been allowed to progress this far in the first place.)

The dilemma, therefore, is not so much whether I can exercise control over the dog, but whether Sally will be able to maintain it. In cases of strong aggression, the trainer must block the behavior. The correction must be utterly overwhelming without being painful and with absolutely accurate timing. The dog must associate the correction with his trainer, so that at future times the trainer's mere threat suffices to quell the aberrant behavior. Much in the same way, drivers quickly observe the speed limit when they see a patrol car. The threat alone of having to pay a fine compels compliant behavior.

Pain would only heighten aggression. A miscalculation on the trainer's part could result in substantial injuries to the other dog or to the trainer himself. For this reason, the remote collar would be a very inappropriate tool. If the dog feels discomfort or even mild pain without being able to locate its source, he will associate it with the other dog and redirect his aggression toward his perceived opponent.

Twenty-five years ago when I started out training dogs for the general public, I naively fell into the trap of thinking that primarily training *dogs* could accomplish this. I expected their owners would quickly recognize the efficacy of my approach and try to emulate it. Only gradually and very reluctantly did I come to accept the undeniable fact that many dog owners are not particularly well-suited for the task of owning a dog, much less of training one. Therefore, it would be useless and could even be harmful to owner and dog to start a process that the owner could not maintain.

"*I* can train him. The question is, can *you* maintain it?" I sum up my ruminations.

"Are you saying the process is not going to be pleasant?" Sally asks doubtfully.

"It could be very ugly and perhaps dangerous," I declare, exaggerating only a little bit. If Sally turns green around the gills now, it is time to backpedal and concentrate on the management of the problem rather than its solution.

"Worse than this?" Sally asks, pointing to her disfigured face again.

"No, probably not," I have to admit.

"Worse than having him euthanized?"

"Definitely not."

"Worse than having him injure or kill another dog or getting himself injured?"

"No, of course not. We are not going to injure him as another large dog probably would. We are not even going to inflict pain. We—"

"Worse than having a lively dog cooped up in a yard and a house for the rest of his life?" Sally is on a roll.

"Certainly not!"

"I will do whatever it takes," she says firmly, and I believe her.

It is indeed easier for me to stop Puck's abominable and perilous behavior than it is for Sally. Not only am I more experienced in dealing with dogs of this caliber, the really decisive advantage lies in the fact that Puck does not know me very well. He will be inclined to be more cautious and to rely less on my support, much in the same way that children are often better behaved at someone else's house. When I come on strong, he *will* feel daunted; if his owner threatened him in the very same way, he might think she was just having a bad day.

For this occasion, I have dressed Puck with a choke chain and a strong leather leash. In normal dog training, fortunately, choke chains have become a thing of the past. In this case, however, I need a means to shut him down should he decide to redirect his aggression toward me. In my hand I have a large plastic Coke bottle in which I have placed an old chain collar, both for weight and for sound. Together, Puck on a loose leash, we approach the fence behind which I have placed another dog. Now timing is of the essence. A split second too late and the exercise is wasted.

As Puck's body stiffens almost imperceptibly, I sense more than I see his aggression kick in. At this precise moment—*before* the aggression has a chance to shoot up and *before* Puck has a chance to act—I descend on him like all furies of hell unleashed. Bellowing at the top of my lungs, which is very loud, I smack him in the face with the plastic bottle several times in quick succession. This, of course, is not going to hurt, but it is sure to intimidate him. Simultaneously, I wade into him, driving him back. Fortunately for me, and I should say for Puck, he makes no attempt to bite me, which speaks for his relative clearheadedness even in a situation like this. He lowers himself, ears glued to his head, and seeks to be comforted. But I am not ready to let him off the hook yet.

Again we approach the fence and I intimidate Puck prophylactically with my voice and by rattling the plastic bottle, but take no further action. Puck evidently believes me when

The Terror of the Neighborhood

I threaten resoundingly that I am ready to murder him and hang him out to dry. When the other dog approaches, Puck shakes like a leaf, but now he is more afraid of displaying aggression than he is of the other dog. While for the moment his fear is better than his usual explosiveness, it is not behavior I wish to encourage. I lead him away without praise and approach the fence again.

Play-acting is a considerable element in dog training. Despite my tempestuous appearance I am keeping a cool head. I am in no way truly angry with Puck or any of the other dogs I train. Nevertheless, in this case I am trying to convey to Puck that I am a madwoman who will stop at nothing. If he believes it, more than half the battle is won.

Puck and I approach the dog behind the fence several more times. As Puck realizes that the other dog is not going to hurt him, he relaxes a bit. *Now* I praise him, sparingly, in a calming voice. Just enough to convey my approval of his newfound neutrality, but not so much that he begins to think I am on his team.

After a short break I repeat the exercise with a different dog behind the fence. As Puck begins to puff himself up, I clonk him on the nose with the plastic bottle and sharply reprimand him, "Cut that out!" *What* I say is far less important than *how* I say it. The tone needs to convey unmistakably that the trainer brooks no dissension. Although this is a clear step down in intensity from the first correction, with any luck it will suffice.

We walk a small circle and approach the fence once more. Puck is tense, but after a moment he deigns to sniff the other dog's nose without trying to bite if off. Of course, I have chosen to place dogs behind the fence who are themselves not very aggressive or energetic, the lovable lumps.

Over the course of the next few days, we repeat the drill

many times with different dogs. By now, Puck has a healthy respect for my formidable powers and I am able to retire the plastic bottle for the time being. When I sense him reacting inappropriately, I warn him, "Behave!" uttered more like a growl than a request. I am the leader and *I* decide when we fight. When he reacts confidently he is praised.

Clearly, there is no way to compel a dog to be friendly. I expect Puck to refrain from starting a fight, not to become an ambassador of canine goodwill.

During the same time span, I also make the recall more reliable with the aid of Thor and secure the Drop at a Distance. These obedience exercises will come in handy when we are ready to take Puck off-leash.

The next step consists in having Puck on a loose leash near another dog. My training partner Betty is approaching with a German Shepherd-Husky mix. Andy is one of our rescued dogs, in training to be civilized enough to be adopted out. She has little obedience, but excruciatingly proper dog manners.

As we approach Andy, not directly but obliquely, in warning I rattle the bottle, now once again purposefully in my hand. A direct approach is often a trigger for aggression. As we pass Andy, Puck pretends she does not exist. This is not good, but can't be helped for the moment.

Why is it not good? Remember, the flip side of avoidance behavior is defensive aggression. What I am hoping to achieve is a semblance of confident behavior.

We approach again, and this time I pause ever so slightly when we are near Andy. Puck turns his head toward her and remains neutral. Before he can change his mind, I walk on, taking him around in a circle. When we pause a second time, Puck sniffs Andy and begins to wag his tail tentatively. Andy graciously licks his nose.

The Terror of the Neighborhood

Once Puck begins to realize that fighting is not an option because a powerful leader *forbids* it, he can start to explore and experience other successful interactions, just as one might crawl through a window if the door is barricaded.

Now—and *only now*—can we begin to "desensitize" Puck. Even the term is poorly chosen in this context. We are actually giving the seed of inborn social behavior a chance to bloom and hope it takes root. Before, it was largely blotted out by the much stronger emotions of fear and aggression.

Puck now meets many different dogs while both are on loose leashes. I realize this is not ideal, but I need to protect the other dog. The sword of Damocles, manifested by my threats, is always hanging over Puck's head, lest he forget that starting a fight is unequivocally prohibited.

Gradually, over many days, Puck's demeanor changes. It is beginning to dawn on him that not every dog is a priori a deadly foe. Now approaches the next and in many ways most daunting hurdle. I want Puck to maintain his relative equanimity when *he* is approached by a strange dog, both of them off-leash. One mistake now and the complete training effort is for naught.

I am planning to take Puck on his first outing in the open space the next day. Sleep eludes me for much of the night as splinters of apprehensive speculation tumble in my brain. This *is* war on my nerves. What if something goes wrong? What if Puck mangles another dog? What if he runs away? There are many uncontrolled dogs. Fortunately, most are friendly, but what if an even slightly hostile or overly boisterous dog accosts Puck? No margin for error here. Is my insurance paid? I don't want to be sued. No other dog trainers I know take these risks. Why am I accepting these dogs with massive behavior problems? I have done this so often, there is nothing left to prove. It's not *my* dog, after all, and all this trepidation is surely not worth the money. There are enough easy dogs to train to keep me busy the rest of my life. What do I care? But of course, that's just it. My attempts at cynicism don't rescue me now. I *do* care. The idea of having Puck locked up in a house and backyard, a gilded prison, for the rest of his life is appalling.

As soon as Puck hops out of the car at the open space and *before* he gets himself into any trouble, Thor strikes him with a bolt of lightning. Puck needs to be convinced that the rules are strictly enforced in this new location as well. Over time this information will generalize, but for now it is best to err on the side of caution. I have abandoned my conspicuous plastic bottle for a throw chain in my hand. If absolutely need be I can smack him with it, but I am hoping that the rattling sound together with my blustering will provide enough of a warning or threat.

After a short while we encounter our first dog. A man with his black Labrador Retriever is walking toward us. The dog is fat and slow and does not seem to pose any real threat. Taking a firm grip on my throw chain, I command, "Down!" and Puck flings himself to the ground. The man calls his dog to him when he sees Puck lying down and she trudges beside him, past Puck and my anxiety. I flash the gentleman a grateful smile.

Puck has been a paragon of good behavior so far, no small thanks to this gentleman who was perceptive enough to restrain his dog when he saw me attempting to control mine. Unfortunately, the majority of owners walking their dogs make no effort (or are unable) to prevent their dogs from running up to just any dog or person. Why one would just naively assume that all dogs are friendly, or that most people won't mind being accosted by a dog, is beyond my imagination.

The Terror of the Neighborhood

Shortly after our first encounter we meet a young couple walking their Labrador mix. As soon as I see them I command Puck to lie down once more. When the owners make no attempt to call their dog back, who is now heading straight for Puck, I release him while rattling the throw chain, with the sharp warning to behave or else! Puck is somewhat uneasy, but makes no attempt to mutilate the Lab mix. I am now halfway convinced that the initial danger is over and walk away quickly, glancing over my shoulder. When the two dogs disengage, I call Puck, who races to catch up with me.

There is, of course, a justification why I release Puck from his Down when another (uncontrolled) dog approaches. Lying down puts a dog in a vulnerable position. Any normal dog will meet another dog on his feet. If a command puts my dog in a disadvantageous or even dangerous situation, it stands to reason that he cannot obey. If the owner frequently issues unreasonable commands, the dog's trust in his or her leadership erodes very rapidly.

On my walk, Puck is not allowed to approach any dog that is kept on a leash. Owners usually have a good reason to keep their dogs tethered. Either the dog is antagonistic toward other dogs or the owner safeguards against losing control. It is only polite not to exacerbate the problem.

Puck is never out of my sight. For now, I keep him with me at a radius of no more than thirty feet. On the trail I call him back *before* he rounds a bend or tops a hill. *I* need to see what he is seeing, so I can intercept Puck's intention if need be. In a few weeks I will let him walk at a maximum radius of about forty to fifty feet, but *always* in sight.

Over the course of the next couple of hours, Puck meets quite a few dogs, many of them uncontrolled, but luckily no hostile ones. Although I stay very vigilant and keep a solid hold on my throw chain, my heart is not pounding wildly every time we meet another dog. With growing experience, Puck becomes noticeably more nonchalant in his dealings with his canine acquaintances.

After several more pleasantly uneventful walks with Puck, it is time to scale the last substantial hurdle, the transfer to Puck's owner. This is for me another anxiety-filled phase in the training process and the one over which I have the least control. Everything now depends on the owner's ability to enforce and maintain the training. If my original assessment of the owner's aptitude was flawed, the laborious process could collapse. If the owner is clumsy or worse, muddleheaded, the dog will relapse and his incipient good habits will be obliterated.

Sally has not been allowed to visit Puck for the several weeks he was in training with me. She is understandably delighted to see him, as is Puck to greet his owner. I have anticipated this, but it is by no means a foregone conclusion. All too frequently, dogs would rather stay here at the kennel than go home with their owners, and while this may be flattering, it also burdens me a great deal. But Sally and Puck fall happily into each other's arms, so to speak.

"Sally, one of the problems is going to be that Puck still considers you part of his support system during his altercations. You have to make clear to him that this is no longer true," I begin.

"Okay," Sally nods, "how do I do that?"

She does not flinch when I describe the procedure with the plastic bottle to her. That is a good sign.

Once more I have deposited a mild-mannered dog behind a secure wire fence. At my request, Sally, plastic bottle in hand, approaches with Puck. After a moment's hesitation

208

The Terror of the Neighborhood

Puck begins to puff himself up. Sally does nothing. There is no time to explain or to be polite. I hurl a second plastic bottle at Puck and bellow something unprintable, before Puck can fall back on his old behavior pattern. Sally is as startled as her dog when I shout at her to return to me—*now!*—before the situation escalates.

"What's wrong, Sally? Were you asleep?" I huff angrily.

"But—but he didn't do anything bad yet!" Sally says defiantly. "Actually, I was rather impressed at how non-aggressive he was. Just a few weeks ago—"

"I *know* what he was like a few weeks ago," I reply a little more calmly. "I'm trying to avoid a relapse. A behavior sequence, once in progress, is very difficult or impossible to interrupt. Sally, you cannot modify behavior *after* it has occurred. A dog who is punished after the fact has learned nothing useful. Next time I want you to descend on Puck as soon as you *sense* him forming the intent."

My little homily is evidently successful. This time Sally bonks Puck on the head with her plastic bottle and shouts at him in time. The correction is not as strong as the one he got from me in the beginning, but, together with the experience of the past weeks, it suffices.

Puck is so flabbergasted that his beloved human has put herself in a position of effective control that he makes no further attempt to be aggressive with a number of other dogs.

Sally is elated. "What a difference! Oh, I'm so proud of him!" she trills over and over again.

But I cut short her rapture. We are not out of the woods yet. My presence clearly had an inhibitory effect on Puck, so that his owner's relatively weak correction was successful. I can only hope that the threat of a strong correction alone will do the trick.

The following day I meet Sally and Puck in the open space.

Barking Up the Right Tree

In the parking area I tell Sally to use Thor's Chain at the very first hint of inattentiveness.

"Already? But he hasn't disobeyed—"

It seems now I have to modify Sally's behavior before *she* falls back on old habits. "Sally!" I admonish. "You have no margin for error!"

"I know, I know!" Sally makes a face. "Before he makes a mistake."

And she rises to the occasion. As her timing improves drastically, so does her confidence in handling her dog. I see Sally frequently, walking Puck off-leash on campus and in the open space, and Puck is the happy gentleman he was meant to be.

Life with
the Schnauzer Family
Call of the Wild

Apache is occasionally getting a little more independent than I wish. She still comes speedily and joyfully most of the time, but when there are squirrels to be pursued, her hearing seems to be deteriorating. I have planned a camping trip to the foothills of the Sierra Nevada anyway, so I take Apache along to give her some much-needed one-on-one time.

In mid-September the vast campground in the woods of Round Valley is all but deserted. Only a few hardy retirees have their gigantic RVs parked at a comfortable distance from me. In the mornings the smell of frying bacon from the kitchens of their rolling houses wafts across the campground, but otherwise I feel blissfully removed from the hurly-burly of a civilized life. But for the wind in the trees and the twittering birds, the silence is complete. The days are still sunny and hot, and far away the retirees are spending lazy hours on the lake in their boats, trolling its murky depths for gullible bass and catfish.

Setting up shelter is not as effortless as I had hoped. Apache, the master thief, absconds with tent pegs and rubber mallet. The things this dog considers useful! Heeding my own advice, I trade her sticks and other items less vital for the pitching of a tent. By the time I have accomplished my chore, the granite tops of the mountains towering over the lake are blazing crimson with the rays of the sinking sun. It is too late now to embark on a hike, so we go for a swim instead. This is a new experience for Apache. Initially, she merely thrashes the water like an eggbeater, using only her front paws. Although this keeps her head above water, it does not accomplish much in the way of locomotion. Nevertheless, she quickly discovers that moving her hind legs as well brings about much more desirable results. Before long she swims with the agility of an otter. If only *I* could learn that fast! I consider it already quite a success if I don't drown.

No camping trip is complete without a campfire. Apache, however, is convinced that every stick I collect for fuel is meant for her amusement. She cannot understand what I could possibly want with an armful of twigs and branches. When my attention wanders she pulls the burning branches out of the fire and carries them around. Before she singes her beard and eyebrows or sets the woods on fire, I unromantically douse the flames with a bucket of water.

Though I'm not normally an early riser, the chill in the tent of this fall morning makes me restless. Apache presses a whiskered ice-cold nose against my cheek and gnaws on my ear. I hug her and with a contented sigh she snuggles up, blissfully nibbling on my nose, not too gently. She clearly enjoys this time alone with me, and appreciates not having to compete for attention.

The squirrels on the pine trees surrounding my tent have started their daily excited chatter. I can see my breath in the cold air and, shivering, I crawl a little deeper under the blankets. Apache shifts her interest to my ear and licks it with great abandon, finally including all of my face. Such morning ablutions are too much even for me.

"Okay, you win; we'll go for a walk."

Call of the Wild

Apache is beside herself. As I attempt to roll out from under my blankets, she leaps on top of me and shows her approval of my decision to end my hibernation by wiggling her little tail like a pendulum gone berserk and kissing me several more times with all the enthusiasm of an adolescent Riesenschnauzer.

Now that I have struggled out of my warm sleeping bag like a giant insect shedding its cocoon, the air seems even chillier. While Apache dances an impatient jig by the tent door, I hastily pull on my sweatsuit and boots and unzip the flap. She streaks out and I follow her at a more indolent pace, pulled as deeply as I can into my hooded sweatshirt, trotting down to the lake.

Once we are in the woods she makes her first acquaintance with Thor. As expected, this experience miraculously blows the rust out of her eardrums. For the next three days, she is always off-leash, and the lesson gets reinforced almost effortlessly.

It is dusk when we come back from a long hike in the mountains. I am very fatigued, but Apache, although she had ceaselessly pursued chipmunks and thrown sticks, would gladly continue. As we approach my very secluded campsite, a man, who ostensibly has been there awhile, pops out from behind my tent.

It's not that I am a Nervous Nellie, I just have a healthy sense of self-preservation and I am alarmed. Apache, however, happily bounds up to the stranger and greets him exuberantly, wiggling and undulating. A fine protector she turned out to be. Damn! Now this guy knows that I am staying here alone with my cream puff of a dog. I wish Ilka were here.

"What are you doing in my camp?" I say gruffly, attempting to banish the tremor from my voice.

The man babbles something about having come up from the town to sell fresh bread.

I can see no bread container, and who needs fresh bread in the dark, anyway? I always thought one sells fresh bread in the morning. And, besides, what was he doing *behind* my tent, and for how long had he been there?

"Well, fine. I don't need any. You're lucky my dog didn't bite you!" I feel like an idiot. Who am I kidding? Surely not this guy. Am I imagining his depraved sneer as he pats my perfidious Apache?

I have to make sure. After the man leaves I retrieve my flashlight and with my stalwart protection dog I make my way to the camp office, which is about a quarter-mile away. The camp warden corroborates the man's story. Yes, they have someone who comes up from town to sell fresh bread. Yes, he usually comes in the mornings or midday. No, they don't understand what he was doing at my campsite. Probably nothing. Shrug.

The reasoning that selling fresh bread somehow indicates a lack of evil intentions is a piece of casuistry that would put any medieval Jesuit to shame.

However, fortunately, the night passes without incident. Beyond doubt, Apache is sleeping much more soundly than I. After all, she has *me* to guard her.

Warts and All

Even when the dog's unsure defensive aggression is directed at people, it is possible in many circumstances to control it. However, this requires persistence and above-average handling skills on the part of the owner.

The annual letter arrived today from Polka. Well, not actually from Polka, but from her owners. It contains, as usual, several pictures, all displaying a large, white, wire-haired, mixed-breed dog with black spots and floppy black ears. Polka, with a tennis ball in her mouth at the beach in Hong Kong, skyscrapers towering at the horizon; Polka, her nose muddy from digging, in front of half-timbered houses in a meadow somewhere in Alsace; Polka, blissfully cavorting in the surf on a beach in Thailand, palm trees in the background; Polka, in the circle of her human family under a Christmas tree. To all appearances a happy, well-adjusted and rather well-traveled dog.

It wasn't always like this. There is nothing in these pictures that betrays how close Polka came to the executioner's needle, because she had rather nastily bitten a woman in the face. That was seven years ago.

"We've decided to try to give Polka another chance. We're willing to pay the twenty-five thousand dollars," Laura sighed, "but not more than once. If you think her behavior can be controlled, we want to try. If not, then ..." Laura trailed off.

This large sum, alas, was not my training fee, but a settlement Laura's family had agreed to pay for the damage Polka had done.

"Describe to me exactly what happened," I said to Laura.

"I was walking Polka on-leash and a woman just approached and started petting her, bending over the dog. I almost thought she was going to kiss her. Polka took offense and snapped at the woman. We'd only had Polka for a couple of days at that time; we had just adopted her from the local animal shelter. I had no idea she would react that way and I couldn't pull her back in time. We weren't told that she had any aggressive tendencies. At the shelter she seemed merely subdued and a little timid."

"You were told she was abused, no doubt," I said, making a face.

Lauren looked surprised. "Yes. How did you know?"

"I've been in the dog-training business for a long time. I have seen a lot of dogs come out of adoption agencies that should never have been devolved on unsuspecting families by people who are sorely lacking knowledge about dog behavior."

Laura nodded, "We would never have adopted her had we known of her aggressive proclivities. And we were going to have her euthanized, but then she had to go through quarantine in our house, and now we have become attached to her. So, if there's something that can be done, we'd like to try."

"Yeah, one does become fond of them, almost against one's will," I reminisced out loud. "I've had nutty dogs too, and have become very attached. I've *loved* them; I just didn't pretend they were *normal*. And I would never be so irresponsible as to breed them or pass them on to an unprepared and gullible new owner."

"Well, we know Polka is not going to be an easy dog.

We'd like to try to learn to control her."

I hadn't even met Polka yet, whom Laura had cautiously left in her car, but I had the strong feeling that if anything could be done, Laura could manage it. Her demeanor was straightforward and there was nothing vague or muddle-headed about her.

"How much damage did Polka do?" I needed to know how serious the dog was.

"Polka broke the skin, but it was really just a scratch. If it had been me, I just would have stuck a Band-Aid on it, but the woman went to the doctor and he filed a dog-bite report. Then we were sued, and now we're settling for a lot of money," Laura reported.

"Your homeowner's insurance doesn't cover it?" It was really none of my business, but I was curious.

"Well, we had just moved here from Europe, and our insurance was not in place yet. Had she bitten the woman a few days later, we'd have been better off." Laura shook her head grimly.

"Laura, if it's any consolation, the woman who approached Polka was an unmitigated blockhead. Approaching and touching a dog without asking the owner is not only foolish, it is bad manners. But sticking your nose into a strange dog's face must surely rank among the dumbest things I've ever heard."

"Perhaps Polka was merely trying to protect me?" Laura glanced at me hopefully, but I could tell by her tone of voice that she doubted this herself.

"Protect you from what, Laura? From a woman coming up to you in a decidedly unthreatening manner? Not a chance! Polka was trying to protect *herself*, and she was more likely to act on her aggression because she felt stronger that there were two of you. Dogs who see boogey men everywhere and danger at every corner are not protective of any one but themselves."

"I thought you'd probably say that," Laura nodded. "There seems to be no question that Polka is very inappropriately aggressive. She has gone after other people, just not with the same dire consequences."

Acknowledging the flaws in a dog's character but being devoted to him in spite of that is a trait I don't very often see in dog owners. I find it an admirable characteristic. Usually, dog owners attempt to explain away deep-seated abnormalities in their dogs' dispositions. This willful blindness prevents them from looking for answers in the right place. Not to mention that these people look like fools to anyone with common sense.

"Has she ever threatened anybody in the family?" I had to ask.

"Oh no, never." Laura shook her head decisively. "She is all sweetness and light at home."

"Well, that at least is good news. Had you answered affirmatively, I probably would have told you to save your money. Let me take a look at the little hoodlum," I instruct her. "Take her out to the training field, on leash. I'll be right there. I want to enter when she is already on the field."

When I opened the gate Polka immediately stiffened, her hackles up. I approached casually, but when I passed her I sensed she was preparing to lunge. I turned to her and Polka backed up stiffly, snarling. If I had given her an opening, she surely would have bitten me. However, instead of avoiding her, I attacked. Charging toward her, I raised my arm as if to strike. She backed up, barking furiously, lips drawn back to expose her teeth. As soon as I turned my back on her, she leapt forward to take advantage of my apparent weakness.

Warts and All

Of course, I was ready for this and wheeled around. Polka stopped and growled.

Clearly, this dog was a walking liability. Her defensive aggression was not confident and therefore close to the surface.

Many people think of aggression per se as something negative. This is not the case. All animals are equipped, to varying degrees, with defensive aggression, the fight-or-flight impulse. They could not survive without it. The element that makes defensive aggression so dangerous is the low threshold or loose trigger that sets off this behavior. Generally, we find low thresholds to aggression in timid, nervous animals. If the unsure aggression results in a bite, it is usually hectic, shallow and not well-aimed. It is as if a fearful, unstrung, panicky person were handed a loaded gun with a hair trigger.

A confident dog, on the other hand, has a moderate or high threshold to aggression. His defensive aggression comes into play only as a last resort. Quite a few police dogs fall into this category. They can be formidable opponents, yet can be trusted in a kindergarten class.

It is not aggression that is the problem, but how well it is contained or containable. I hang out the garlic and the crosses when I encounter skittish, nervous dogs. There is no need to be uneasy with self-confident ones.

"Laura, not to put too fine a point on it, Polka is a typical fear-biter," I summed up my observation so far.

"Yes, she is," said Laura, "I think you are right. That's probably why her previous owner gave her up. She had become too much of a liability."

Ah, the pleasure of working with someone whose feelings of self-worth are not wrapped up in her dog. Quite a few people would rather face the specter of excommunication and being boiled in puppy chow in purgatory than have any aspersions cast on their dogs.

"All right, let's see what else she is," I said picking up the Puppy Fishing toy.

When I made the ball at the end of the string fly, Polka was instantly drawn into the chase. When she caught the ball I could play tug-o'-war with her and even approach and stroke her. It was as if she had completely forgotten that she had just threatened to bite my posterior if I were not so peskily confrontational.

"The previous owners must have played with her, because she is comfortable once she has a tennis ball in her mouth. That's very good news. The ball is a signal for security," I explained to Laura.

"She is also aggressive with other dogs. She behaves with dogs the same way as with people."

"You mean she blusters and tries to get in a cheap shot if she can?" It was a statement more than a question.

"Exactly," Laura nodded.

"We need to take a look at that as well, before I can give you a verdict."

I led Polka up to a dog behind a wire fence. Polka never so much as made a peep. She clearly was a little daunted by me and probably thought it wise to keep her priorities straight. Even when I had Betty approach her with another dog, Polka did not dare to show any aggression. That was a good sign, because it meant that Polka was able to control herself under compulsion.

Next, I put Polka through a series of leash corrections. I needed to see if she responded calmly or if she would come flying up the leash and try to latch on to my arm. I could handle this, but Laura could not. Fortunately, Polka reacted as reasonably and predictably as one might expect from an untrained dog, and I rewarded her with a thrown ball to lift her spirits.

"I think you can learn to get this problem under control. Emphasis on control, because her propensity to take advantage of weakness in strangers can be minimized, but it is not going to go away."

"You hear that?" Laura asked her dog, rubbing Polka's floppy black ears. "There is hope for you." Relief flooded Laura's face as she smiled at me self-consciously. "The whole family is in love with this dog. It would be a hard blow for my son in particular to have to give her up," she said by way of explanation and blew her nose.

The first phase of Polka's training consisted merely in teaching her the Rocket Recall, the Sit and the Down with positive motivation, namely, food, balls and lots of praise and stroking. This took several weeks. Once Polka opened up, I certainly had to agree that she was a charming dog— when she wasn't in the process of biting someone. Because she had plenty of prey behavior and adored playing with balls and was a voracious eater, she became an avid and quick learner. Laura was a reasonably competent teacher.

"You understand that the skills Polka learns through positive motivation do not actually amount to control in her case, don't you?" I cautioned her. "Do not take any chances with her. Keep her on leash and walk her where you aren't likely to encounter any people or dogs. And you must anticipate what people around her are about to do."

"Believe me, I'll never let anyone approach her again!" Laura shook herself like a wet poodle.

When I began to demand the Down from Polka, she revealed herself as rather headstrong and insensitive but, luckily for her and for us, she never even thought of being aggressive with me or her owner.

"She really is stubborn," Laura observed as she was sweating it out with Polka and came up for air. "She is so timid, I thought surely she would give in easily."

"Timid and nervous do not necessarily mean submissive. Many, if not most, confident dogs are remarkably compliant. I would surmise that Polka got some of her lack of tractability from her Dalmatian forbears."

Appropriate consistency and firmness proved, as almost always, successful. When the penny finally dropped and Polka realized that resistance was not in her best interest, she enjoyed obedience training once more.

With Polka's fiery disposition, obedience had to be absolute in order to be able to give her the freedom she needed for her mental and emotional health. We secured the recall with the aid of a remote collar and Thor's Chain.

When we met in the parking lot of the open space, Laura's customary pluck had all but abandoned her. "I hardly slept last night," she confessed. "I am terrified that something will go wrong."

"Is your insurance paid up?" I quipped.

But she was not in the mood for insouciant jest. Her hands were shaking when she put the remote collar on Polka.

"Ready?" I asked.

Laura swallowed and nodded valiantly.

"Where is the remote control?" I didn't see it in Laura's hand.

"Oh," Laura said, "I think I left it in the car." She rummaged through her car and emerged with disheveled hair and troubled eyes. "I must have left it at home—I think."

This woman was in no condition to lead any dog, much less Polka.

"Okay, Laura," I said to her, "we'll switch to plan B. *I'll* handle Polka from now on, for the next several walks. You simply accompany me."

"I'd like that," she declared, still tense.

I put my own remote collar on Polka and we headed for the woods.

Although I kept a tight rein on her, figuratively speaking, Polka had the time of her life. Each time a jogger came into view on the horizon she had to drop into the Down position, but once the jogger had safely passed, I threw a ball as a reward. She was uneasy with other dogs, but not outright hostile.

We successfully repeated the walks at the park, the beach and in different regions of open space. Encouraged by the many successful endeavors, Laura was able to take over.

A year after graduation, Laura brought a very happy and well-adjusted Polka to our kennel for an extended stay.

"Neither my husband nor my son use the remote collar anymore," Laura reported. "Polka is very obedient, although we do watch her carefully. We know that her fiery personality is not going to change completely. I am more cautious. I like to have the collar on her when we go out, just in case, although I almost never have to use it."

Polka's pictures, among many others, are tacked up on our rogues' gallery at the kennel office. Tanya, the German Shepherd who used to hate and attack children, shown with the brand new baby, the dog blissfully licking his face; Tanya three years later, a smiling toddler in cowboy boots and rather too large jeans, holding onto her ruff. Rocky, the Rottweiler who was dog aggressive, enthusiastically chasing a ball at the dog park. Chloe, the Labrador who used to run away, camping with her family, no leash in sight. Dixie, the Dobermann, stretched out next to her owner's desk in an office. So many former problem dogs, reclining on couches, wearing funny hats or lying under Christmas trees.

Sometimes, when a particularly thickheaded owner or a seemingly intractable problem behavior exasperates me, looking at these pictures gives my mood a lift.

Life With the Schnauzer Family

Fly-Boy

The biggest reward for me of having a well-trained dog consists of my ability to integrate him or her into my life more fully. Call me a tad eccentric, but I think a companion dog should accompany his owner as much as possible. What a dreadfully mind-numbing and miserable life for a dog to be sequestered in house and yard, interrupted only by brief walks while tied to a short leash!

My next trip leads me to St. Louis to attend the annual Schnauzer Fest of the Working Riesenschnauzer Federation. This time it is Ammo's turn to be the special dog.

Flying with a dog is always somewhat nerve-wracking for me. It is only a four-hour flight, but a lot can go wrong. I choose a direct flight that takes off and lands at a cool time of day. During the flight the baggage compartment is climatized, but while the airplane sits on the runway the temperatures can easily and quickly rise to lethal levels. (A few airlines, like Lufthansa, specialize in animal transports. Their baggage compartments are usually air-conditioned or heated even when the plane is standing.)

When I check in, I make known to the airline that I have a dog with me and I would like to be advised when he is on the plane. I am not going to sit down unless I am assured that my dog is safely on board. I don't want Ammo to be shipped to Tibet by mistake. Nor do I want to exit my

225

plane in St. Louis, only to find that Ammo in his crate is still sitting on some baggage cart in the midday sun in San Francisco! I have heard many horror stories of people who were too naively trusting. Some airline officials are more accommodating than others, but I do my best to be polite, firm and persistent.

"The captain just informed me that your dog is on board, Ms. Reeves," the flight attendant notifies me with a professional smile. "You can sit down now."

I do, although I am not at ease until I have Ammo back.

Managing a large dog, an oversized crate and a suitcase in an airport is no small feat. I am therefore much relieved when I spy my friend Ann, who has come to pick me up and take me to the car-rental place where I hope a minivan awaits me.

There are lots of seats in the minivan and no room for the crate.

"I don't want all these seats. I need you to take at least one of them out."

"No can do that," the attendant says in broken English.

"When I made reservations I mentioned that I needed no back seats but lots of storage room in the van. The office person assured me that this could be arranged," I insist.

"No can do that," the man repeats.

"But the van is no good to me if I can't put my dog crate in it," I say a trifle irritated, leaning across the counter of the tiny glass house in which he is sitting.

The man shakes his head stubbornly.

What am I supposed to do? Put wheels on the crate and pull it like a trailer?

"I have a big dog. Look!" With these fateful words I pat my hand on the counter, intending for Ammo to put his paws on it and corroborate my claim. Ammo feels sprightly after his enforced five-hour rest, and instead of putting his paws *on* the counter he flies *over* it, right into the little glass booth, which he just about fills up.

Ammo gives a friendly wiggle of his tail and peers up at the attendant inquisitively. Maybe the human is going to reward him with a cookie for this feat. The man, however, presses himself against the wall, his eyes bugging out of his head. My friend Ann pretends she doesn't know me, and I admit, I am a tiny bit embarrassed.

Getting Ammo out again is quite an endeavor. The door to the booth is locked from the inside, and there is no way the attendant is going to squeeze by my dog, who of course has no intention of jumping back over the counter. He is, after all, just an adolescent and does not really know how to clear this high a jump. It was all a fortunate accident.

"I trow you de key," the man says faintly, gaping at the big, black, bearded devil in front of him and surreptitiously making the sign to ward off the evil eye.

Once Ammo is again safely with me, there still remains the problem of the superfluous seat.

"As I was saying, I have a big dog and—"

"I take de seat out, okay? Jus' hol' your dog. Go over dere," with a trembling hand the attendant points to a corner at the far side of the hall.

Who am I not to oblige him?

Showdown!

Uncontrolled social aggression, particularly if it is directed against the dog's owner, is in many ways the ugliest and most dangerous behavior. It does not spring from fear, but from a feeling of competition or dominance, and always denotes a profound lack of respect for the owner.

"You'd better call Christine," said Betty as I stumbled into the office with my obligatory gallon mug of coffee. "She's left three messages already, trying to reach you this morning. She sounded pretty upset."

I believe early mornings are for birds and worms. But even in my befuddled state I recognized that this urgency was not typical for Christine. Christine and Eric have brought their two dogs, a six-year-old castrated Old English Sheep Dog named Harley and a medium-sized brown crossbred dog named Mickey, to the kennel for many years. They are among our best and best-liked clients.

"Damn! I bet Harley has bitten them," I voiced my intuition. Harley had never given us any trouble at the kennel, but as a typical representative of his breed, his willful disposition was unmistakable.

Taking a big gulp of European-strength coffee to kick-start my brain, I dialed Christine's number.

"Hi, Christine, what's up?"

"Harley bit Eric and me rather badly yesterday," Christine told me, a distinctive tremor in her voice. "Both of us had to be sewn up at the emergency ward. I will not live with a dog of whom I have to be afraid and we are prepared

229

to have him euthanized. It breaks my heart, though. We really love this dog."

I have heard this cliche many times, and I usually don't give much credence to it. In Christine's case, however, I knew it to be true. No one could be more devoted to their dogs, to whom they refer as "the boys," than Eric and Christine. The unwillingness to live with a dog who is likely to inflict serious injury seems to me quite reasonable.

"Slow down, Christine. Tell me what happened."

"I wanted to put him out in the yard yesterday, because we had visitors coming. I know he doesn't like it, but usually he complies reluctantly for a cookie or if I speak sternly to him. This time he refused. When I took him by the collar to lead him out, he bit me very badly in the arm. When Eric tried to take him outside, Harley also bit him severely."

Christine is not given to overwrought hyperbole and I believed her when she said severely.

"We've long known that he was building up to this because he growls at us whenever he doesn't like to do something. I've already made an appointment for euthanasia this afternoon," Christine went on. "I think it's better not to drag this out. Eric has devolved this on me. He agrees, but he says he can't do it." Now Christine was crying.

I gave her time to collect herself and she continued, "I want to know if there is anything we can do, anything at all to prevent it from happening again."

"You've got two options," I offered. "You can learn to manage the problem by avoiding situations that might set him off. But that means that you have to dance around his temper tantrums. In the long run, the behavior will actually get worse. Pretty soon you will have to ask his permission to sit on your couch."

"No, I don't want to live like that. I don't want to get

used to the threat of getting injured by my dog."

"Or you can teach him that he loses when he attacks you. This is clearly a dominance struggle. Let me warn you, the success rate is exceedingly low."

"I'll do anything," Christine said hopefully.

"If you fail, the problem will become worse than before. And even if you succeed, you quite probably will be bitten at least a couple of times in the process. And it has to be accomplished by you. You wouldn't benefit if I did it for you."

"What do I have to do? I'll do it," Christine said without hesitation.

"In cases of minor dominance aggression, particularly in young dogs, ignoring, but in no way deferring to the dog, works best," I began my oration. "But—"

"Harley is six years old," Christine interrupted.

"I know. In your case the problem is *way* past the ignoring cure. You have to counterattack your dog and win that fight, maybe more than once, just as a superior dog would do. In the process, unfortunately, the stakes are raised. That means he will do what he can to maintain his position. It could be very dangerous, and if you lose, you'll be worse off than before."

"My appointment to have him euthanized is this afternoon. What could be worse than that?"

Generally, I believe firmly that if the owners have to subdue their dog by harsh physical means, the dog is not the right animal for them. If Harley had been my dog, for example, the situation would never have spun out of control this far. I would have reminded Harley, at the first sign of social aggression, that such behavior would not be tolerated; and unquestionably, I would have made my point so that it registered!

Barking Up the Right Tree

In desperate cases, however, when the life of the dog or the health of the owner is at stake, I am willing to resort to other tactics, if I can sense determination in the owner. Nevertheless, if the owners are weak, I would concentrate on the management of the problem, teaching them how to avoid being injured.

"All right, let's use a two-pronged approach. For the next several months, he is not to be fed from a bowl. Make him come to you and feed him in small increments from your hand. If he ignores you, he doesn't eat. He could stand to lose some weight, anyway. Other than that, don't change his daily routine, but minimize the attention you give him.

"Secondly, I want you to manage the biting problem by avoiding situations that might lead to an altercation. Nothing is worse than being caught off guard. When you and Eric are ready, you need to provoke an incident. When Harley threatens you or bites you, you must attack. Do what you can to avoid injuring him, but with this exclusion, anything goes. You may bonk him with a plastic bucket, and you may use a large plastic garbage-can lid like a Roman shield. Make a lot of noise. Throw pots and pans on the floor and act as if you had gone berserk. Let him think that you can cause the walls of Jericho to tumble and the earth has come to swallow him up."

"We'll do it!" Christine said decisively.

"It is imperative that you make the point to Harley in such a way that it reaches him the first, or at the very least the second time. You are not going to win a prolonged dominance struggle." I left no doubt about the severity of the confrontation. "And cancel your appointment at the vet's."

Two weeks went by and I heard nothing from Christine. I was tempted to call, but decided against it. Either Harley was dead or the struggle for dominance had not yet taken place. In either case there was nothing I could do to help. This was Christine and Eric's decision; it was not my place to influence them in either direction.

Finally after about three weeks, Christine called.

"I just wanted to thank you," she gushed. "It's going beautifully. Every time we tell Harley to do something, he lowers his head and complies. He hasn't been this obedient since he was very young."

"You had it out with him?"

"Twice," Christine chuckled with pride in her voice. "The plastic bucket works really well. The second time he got quite nasty, so Eric and I sat on him for about half an hour. We sat on him! Can you believe it? He was struggling so hard, but eventually he gave up. He has been like a lamb since that time."

"You weren't bitten?" I was incredulous.

"Oh, yes!" Christine said cheerfully, "But, you know, it was worth it. He is a completely different dog. He is actually—polite."

That was six years ago. Harley never again forgot his manners or challenged Christine or Eric. To his owners' great sorrow, he was eventually euthanized at the age of twelve years due to an age-related debilitating spinal disease.

There is another approach to dealing with aggression against the owner: The dog is isolated in a run for weeks or even months at a time. He receives no human or animal contact at all and is merely fed once or twice a day. After the first couple of weeks, depending on the severity of the dog's transgression, he is asked to comply with his owner. The minutest sign of disobedience sends the dog back into solitary incarceration.

Although the method often shows a certain measure of

success, I am strongly opposed to it. It may *seem* more benign than physical punishment, but solitary confinement is the most cruel punishment there is for dogs with strong social needs. Those dogs whose social behavior is weak in the first place will merely learn that they *really* don't need people, after all, and become even more dangerous than before.

Victim? Victoria!

If a dog is properly raised within a clearly defined social structure, he learns to fit in, because early on, his superiors drive the point home that they do not tolerate antisocial behavior. Once a dog has become a bully, inappropriate leniency and all the cookie training in the world will not reach the root of the problem behavior.

The elderly woman looks up at me disconsolately. Her Beagle, Mork, had just snapped at her for the umpteenth time during my obedience class.

"Edna, don't look at *me*. If you don't correct him in a way that registers, he is going to get worse and worse. I've explained that to you a hundred times." Patience may be a virtue sometimes, but with irresolute dog owners, forbearance accomplishes nothing. On the contrary, these people would continue to dither endlessly.

"I know," nods Edna unhappily, but there is no change in her demeanor.

"Look at your son. He has Maxwell well under control. Look what a nice dog Maxwell has become in a short time," I continue to pressure poor Edna.

Edna and her son Harry had adopted Mork and Maxwell, the terrible Beagle brothers. The dogs were nasty, spoiled specimens, bad-tempered with other dogs, but particularly belligerent toward their owners whenever they were expected to do something they disliked. With my help, Harry had taught Maxwell that certain behavior was not tolerated. In just a few weeks Maxwell changed from a vile, obnoxious bully into a nice, fairly obedient little fellow.

Not wanting to neglect my other students, I leave pathetic Edna and odious Mork to their fate for the moment. Few things are more distasteful to me than prodding irresolute owners to be firm.

In the obedience class, Edna is falling further and further behind, because every time she demands obedience, her dog threatens her. Generally, I acknowledge that it is nearly always impossible to change the behavior of people who have become victims of their dogs. However, I am willing to give this problem one more try. Therefore, I ask Edna to meet me for a private lesson.

When she is alone with me Edna opens up. "I have such a horror of physical abuse," she confides. "I was abused as a child and I just can't be hard on Mork. I know he is a nasty dog." She is not fishing for excuses, merely offering an explanation.

"Maybe Mork is not the right dog for you," I voice my doubts. "You already adopted him with these social aggression problems. He was probably pampered and always won out when he intimidated his owners until they got tired of it and passed the problem on to some unsuspecting soul."

"I wouldn't want to act that irresponsibly," says the ever-so-considerate Edna.

It is time to be blunt. "Edna, I don't have to live with this nasty dog of yours. If you want to be injured by your own dog, that is your prerogative and we can end this conversation right here. But let me just tell you this: If Mork lived in a dog pack, there is no way he would be allowed this antisocial behavior. He would have to pay a heavy price, perhaps in blood. He is not a leader; he is a bully. By comparison to what another *dog* would do to him, anything we do to change his behavior is going to be child's play. There is a difference between abusing a dog and stopping him from viciously injuring you."

Edna squirms like an eel. "I know you're right, but I have to think this over. I have to be ready for this."

"Of course. It's your dog and your life. Let me know if you want to continue."

Frankly, I don't expect that Edna will see the light and take control of this situation. But I am wrong.

A few days later Edna calls. "I've given this a great deal of thought, and I want to go ahead with the training." There is no trace of doubt in her voice.

Once Edna has made up her mind, she surprises even me. In the face of her now-resolute approach, bully Mork doesn't stand a chance. In just a few weeks, Mork performs even better than his brother Maxwell in my class. And, what is more important, he now likes and respects Edna.

For several months I hear nothing from Edna. Then a letter from her arrives. She writes that at the time of training Mork she was involved in a rather nasty lawsuit concerning some property. Edna had chosen not to fight and let her relatives get the better of her. However, once she had successfully overcome the hurdle of making her dog respect her, she used her newfound fortitude to stop her relatives from taking advantage of her and won the lawsuit.

The letter ends, "Training my dog taught me that I *can* take charge. I learned to stand up for myself. Thank you."

Life With
the Schnauzer Family

As Ye Sow, So Shall Ye Reap:
Travels With Apache

It has finally happened. A member of the Working Riesenschnauzer Federation of America has qualified to compete at the annual Schutzhund World Championships for Riesenschnauzer, which is to take place in Saxony, in the former East Germany, this year. Storm, the handler, with Iro, her dog, are to represent the United States at this rather prestigious event. (As I have mentioned before, Schutzhund is an international dog sport. It takes the form of a triathlon, with tracking, obedience and agility, as well as a simulated protection phase.)

I'm overdue for a vacation, so I plan to be part of the support team. Apache gets to accompany me. She is now nearly two years old, has started her Schutzhund training and is very lively. Although she has had scant formal obedience training, she is properly socialized, and by that I mean she has learned the appropriate behavior in social situations and she accepts me as the inspired and trustworthy leader. This alone makes her very manageable in all situations.

We meet in Berlin, a few days before the event, to acclimate Iro and to partake of some training sessions one of the local Riesenschnauzer clubs is providing for us. Us being Storm and her husband Bill; Gerald, another member of the

239

Barking Up the Right Tree

American cheerleading contingent, sans dog; and I with Apache.

As much as I have become Americanized and prefer to live in the United States, I miss the relatively tolerant, often quite supportive, attitude of many Europeans toward dogs. Even after a spate of mostly politically motivated laws and regulations concerning so-called fighting dogs, it is still infinitely easier in Germany to take dogs to most places, travel with dogs, and provide them with the necessary off-leash exercise than it is in America. Dogs, and that unequivocally means well-controlled dogs, are allowed practically everywhere, with the possible exception of hospitals, theaters, churches and grocery stores. (The unwillingness of many Europeans to clean up after their dogs is less endearing, however. These owners have elevated the skill of staring into space while their dogs relieve themselves on public streets and in parks to an art form.) A training degree called the "companion dog" that includes a temperament test and off-leash control is nicknamed the "driver's license for dog owners." Training for it is offered at little or no cost everywhere.

After a fitful, jet-lagged night on my part and a contented snooze on my dog's, the phone rings at the ungodly hour of six a.m.

"We're going tracking," the voice of Volker, the training director of our host Riesenschnauzer club, trumpets forth from the receiver into my reluctant ear. "We'll pick you up in half an hour," he adds gleefully.

"I didn't bring any rubber boots," I say lamely, fumbling for my glasses. Damn these training fanatics!

"We'll bring you some," Volker informs me. "What size do you wear?"

It's no use. Besides, the honor of the Americans is at stake.

Travels With Apache

When we arrive at the tracking area, mowed and plowed fields moist with morning dew, Storm and Iro are already at work. Iro is toiling attentively, following the track of about two thousand paces methodically, footstep by footstep. Unfailingly, he points out the "lost" articles by lying down. If he performs this well at the championships, he'll place high.

Apache thinks her puppy-level track is a snap. Finding slices of hot dogs in deep footprints is fun; it certainly is not work! California born and raised, she is used to much more difficult tracking conditions: arid, dusty fields and an owner who functions with diminished capacity in the mornings and therefore often trains in the heat of the afternoon.

Training resumes after lunch at the club's training field. Much to the amazement and envy of the Americans, we are told that in most places in Germany, dog owners have a tremendous choice of training facilities. Within a half-hour driving radius, one typically has access to at least a dozen training areas, often on the outskirts of town. The cities provide long-term use of property for a pittance. The club erects a club home for shelter and the members become effective stewards of the land thus leased. If this were only possible in America! I believe the incidences of dog bites and of dogs killed in traffic would be reduced drastically and animal shelters would have to euthanize far fewer dogs. (Oh well, I can dream, can't I?) By contrast, it is not uncommon for an American training enthusiast to have to drive two or more hours to find a single, usually privately owned, training facility with competent trainers.

After a successful obedience session, Volker announces that the protection phase will take place in the city forest to make it more interesting for the dogs. The Americans are flabbergasted. In the park? Is this man crazy?

Barking Up the Right Tree

"I think he is serious," Gerald groans. "Remember last year when he judged the companion dog trial in St. Louis?"

The Americans turn ashen and nod.

"He marched all the contestants through a department store. Nine Riesenschnauzer, for chrissakes. People couldn't have been staring more if we all had danced through the aisles in pink tutus."

"So?" Volker joins the conversation with irrefutable logic. "What good is a companion dog if he does not learn to accompany you?"

After training, Volker announces that we are now all going for a companionable walk, as is the custom with this club. This means eight or nine handlers and their dogs.

"You mean, all the dogs off-leash? I don't know—" Storm isn't trusting her ears. She is suffering from culture shock.

"What's the matter, you can't control Iro off-leash on a walk?" Volker asks condescendingly. This is, of course, nonsense, and he knows it. Few dogs are better controlled than Iro.

It is rather a spectacle. Eight Riesenschnauzer, always kept at a radius of no more than twenty-five yards from their owners, forage and root around for mice. When a jogger approaches, the forest resounds from the shouted command *"Platz!"* and all the dogs drop as one and lie motionless until released. At the lake we meet various other owners with their dogs, who seem nearly equally well-controlled. In addition, the forest is crawling with people just out for a stroll. Everyone is getting along just fine. The willingness and ability to control their dogs, as well as a modicum of thoughtfulness on the dog owners' side and a little bit of tolerance on the part of the dogless people, seem to work wonders.

I can't wait to take Apache on trains and buses and therefore decline the offer of a lift back to my hotel. In front of a camera store near the tram station, I spy a colossal hand-painted sign above a voluminous tub of water that reads: "Dog Filling Station." Somehow, I don't think I would encounter a similar arrangement on the streets of San Francisco. At least I never have. While Apache takes a sip and I grope for my camera, the storeowner appears from behind the counter for a chat and to give Apache a friendly pat. Before I catch my tram, I take a picture of Apache at the Filling Station and buy several roles of film from this Good Samaritan.

Dogs ride for the price of a child's ticket. It is a wholly agreeable experience. No one stares, no one seems afraid, and Apache behaves as if riding public transport is old hat to her.

After a lengthy hot shower, I feed Apache and we set out to find a nice place for my dinner. It is one of the few balmy evenings in Berlin and walking is a pleasure. Perhaps because Berlin was a political island for so long, green abounds. Nowhere (except in the former East Berlin) is there a hint of the concrete desert one expects in so large a city.

Fewer and fewer restaurants offer genuine German cuisine these days, and a good thing it is, too. One does tire so of schnitzel, fried potatoes and overcooked vegetables in a sticky sauce! After perusing the outside menu I decide on an Italian garden restaurant and choose a large table under a leafy tree studded with lanterns.

"Would your dog like some water?" the waiter inquires.

"What?" I stammer, stunned out of my manners. Am I hearing right? "Oh no, thank you," I rally, "but I'll have the spaghetti con frutti di mare and a glass of white wine, please."

The waiter brings a bowl of water, anyway. This man knows how to get himself a large tip!

An elderly couple enter the garden and look around

searchingly. There is only one empty table left, near the street. They make for my table.

The waiter intercepts them. "No, not there. There's a dog under the table."

Good. Go away. I'm not in a gregarious mood.

"A dog?" The man lifts the tablecloth and peers under the table at Apache. "A Riesenschnauzer! Come, Traudi! We'll sit here!" he heralds in the general direction of his wife. And to me, "We have a Riesenschnauzer, too."

The waiter shrugs ostentatiously, I more inwardly. There goes my quiet evening. Might as well make the best of it, I think grumpily.

Several hours and a bottle of wine later, near midnight, a sudden rainsquall cuts short our most pleasant exchange of dog stories. Meeting interesting people is indeed a gratifying fringe benefit of having a canine companion.

A Beggar
in a Heartless Land

With clumsy training attempts, the owner may frighten the dog and unwittingly tap into the dog's defensive aggression. Just as it is possible to foster the dog's compliance through decisive but compassionate leadership, it is possible to create resistance through harsh and insensitive treatment.

Trucker, the young German Shepherd Dog in my office, is somewhat timid and nervous. Clearly, he is not a paragon of stable disposition, but he is not crazed, either.

Unlike his owner.

"As I told you on the phone, he is BITING us. He's BITING me, he's BITING my husband, and he GROWLS when we come near his food." Michelle's voice is rising in pitch until she ends in a screech.

I know from long and tedious experience that there are only two ways in which I can hope to connect with Michelle's brain. I could cut through her extreme agitation with a mighty thunderbolt or I can let her run dry. It's been a long day; therefore, I choose the latter. Affecting a slightly bored expression, I cross my legs and fold my hands in my lap with a sigh and listen to her fulmination, without offering any pearls of wisdom or indicating in any other way interest or disapproval.

Finally, Michelle is emotionally depleted and running out of oxygen.

"How old is Trucker?" I ask dispassionately.

Barking Up the Right Tree

"Ten months," Michelle says and siphons in a big draught of air, probably in preparation for another febrile iteration.

Making a peremptory gesture to forestall further outbursts, I am eventually able to extricate a sufficiently coherent case history.

Michelle and her husband both want to prevent their dog from becoming dominant. To this end, they chase Trucker when he has picked up an unapproved item, such as a sock or a Kleenex, and take it away from him. His growing evasiveness, namely running away or playing keep-away when he has stolen a sock or other item, is attributed to his stubbornness, dominance and lack of loyalty. Michelle and her husband also think it imperative that they be able to take food away from Trucker at any time. Both exercise this right frequently.

At the age of nine months Trucker, when backed into a corner or approached when he was eating, started to growl. To quell this so-called dominance, Michelle's husband wrestled Trucker to the ground, rolling him on his back and holding him there while screaming at him. The next time he tried to punish the dog in this way, Trucker snapped at him. Now it is impossible to reach for Trucker when he is eating or has something in his mouth without the risk of being bitten.

Anytime I am dealing with a biting dog, I must analyze the predominant motivation behind this action. Although to the superficial observer all biting behavior may seem alike, it stands to reason that I have to treat the problem of insecurely defensive or fear biting differently from biting that is meant to establish dominance and, likewise, deal with prey-play biting in a different way than with aggressive biting.

"Dominance on Trucker's part has little or nothing to do with his behavior. It is actually you who are abusing your dominance over him. You are putting him in a position where he feels he has to defend himself against you," I say sternly to Michelle, who for once doesn't know what to say next.

"But—" she opens and shuts her mouth like a carp out of water, gulping for air.

Before she can launch into an incensed and prolix justification of her behavior, I take advantage of the lull. "It is perfectly normal for a dog to want to keep his find or his food. By your excessively demanding his submission, you foster resistance and avoidance behavior. You punish the slightest resistance by putting Trucker in fear for his life! Now he is afraid and thinks he has to defend *himself* when you even come near his food. His behavior has very little to do with disobedience and everything to do with your inappropriate punishment and persecution of him."

These are strong words, but I think they are justified. Nietsche said, "Distrust all in whom the impulse to punish is powerful," and in this regard I agree with him wholeheartedly. Some owners accuse their dogs of being dominant to mask their own fixation on excessive subjugation. I believe that these people are, deep down, so afraid of their dogs that any attempt by the dog to assert his individuality is seen as a threat to them. Instead of becoming benign and intelligent leaders, they become bullies.

In reality, strong dominance behavior against humans is quite rare with domestic dogs. Most domestic dogs readily accept, and indeed crave, reasonable leadership. Domestic dogs have self-selected, for many thousands of years, for the retention of juvenile characteristics. In a sense, they never really grow up in comparison to their wild relatives. There is no such thing as an obedient adult wolf, at least not as compared to a domestic dog.

"But—shouldn't we be able to take things away from

Trucker? After all, they aren't *his* things, they are *ours!*" Michelle bleats, a little less sure of herself now.

This would be funny, of course, if the poor beggar of a dog didn't have to suffer so as a result of this imbecilic and unfeeling attitude.

"Being able to take something away from Trucker and tormenting him with your ideas of obedience are two different issues. You have to earn his trust before you can put demands on him. Your demands have to be reasonable. And furthermore, if you have to physically subdue Trucker, he is probably not the right dog for you." I keep my voice flat and dispassionate, in order not to give Michelle's volatile emotions a target.

"So what do you suggest? We should just let him run the house?" The unpleasant metallic inflection edges back into Michelle's voice.

Unpleasant for me and probably even more unpleasant for Trucker's sensitive hearing. Trucker is giving the appearance that all this does not concern him. He ostentatiously has turned his back to us and not once has he made any attempt to communicate with his owner.

Endeavoring to answer calmly, I explain as if to a sick and not very bright toddler, "No, that's not what I'm saying at all. Trucker has to trust you before he can give you obedience, and you have to learn to understand him before you can earn his trust. There are no quick fixes. You would have to train him correctly, so he learns not to fear and despise you."

My attempt to be reasonable is met with shrill laughter. "Trust!" Michelle is positively swelling with pious indignation. "*He* bites *us! We* can't trust *him!* So you say there's nothing we can do."

"No, I'm saying you have to spend some time and energy to train him."

It's no use. This woman is not going to change her behavior. I'd like to throw her out of my office. Instead, I rise and say, "I have another appointment. Think it over and let me know if you want to proceed with training."

A few weeks later Michelle calls to cancel a reservation for Trucker at the kennel. "We gave him back to the breeder. He was just getting too vicious."

Poor Trucker.

Dysfunction du jour

These days we hear a lot about so-called separation anxiety. It has become a catchall term for a variety of behavioral syndromes. Unquestionably, when a dog exhibits profound separation anxiety, all the early mistakes in training and raising the dog have come home to roost.

Just when I think I have seen it all, some client invents a new folly.

I am waiting at the gate to my training field for Janet to get her dog. Tigger is a female yellow Labrador mix of medium size, about three years old.

Janet hoists Tigger out of her car and carries her to the training field. I can barely believe my eyes and can't wait to hear her explanation. But she is not offering any. She merely sets Tigger down and looks at me expectantly.

I have to ask, "Why were you carrying your dog?"

"Tigger doesn't know how to walk on a leash," Janet says, dead serious.

I can't help it. I am laughing so hard that I have difficulty standing up. Wiping away my tears I snort, "You need a backpack so you can carry her like a baby."

Janet is a little taken aback by my paroxysms of mirth and gives me a chagrined smile, "That's why we're here. I need help. I can't take her anywhere, because she won't walk on a leash and I can't leave her, because she destroys the house when I'm gone."

"And you can't crate her, because she refuses to go into a crate, right?"

251

Barking Up the Right Tree

"Yes!" Janet exclaims. "Exactly! How did you know?"

Good Lord! How could I *not* know. But I say politely, if somewhat nebulously, "Oh, you know, intuition and experience," waving my hand wearily.

Meanwhile, Tigger sits next to her owner, cowering and deferential. She constantly tries to appease Janet by licking her hand or jumping at her in a clinging fashion. Tigger cringes when I touch her, but makes no attempt to bite.

I propose to begin by teaching Tigger that legs are for walking. "This seems like a reasonable starting point. It's hard to train her if she won't walk with you. Please have a seat while I work with her."

When I take the leash Tigger stands rooted to the ground. Coaxing her with treats or a toy has no effect. But unlike her owner, I have no intention of carrying her. I tighten the leash and take a step, prepared to drag Tigger if I must. She is wearing a normal buckle collar. As soon as the leash becomes taut, however, Tigger has a conniption fit. She squeals as if she were being skinned alive and flops on the line like a fighting trout on a hook. I have anticipated this and merely hold the leash steady without yanking it or intervening in any way. Fighting Tigger at this time, jerking the leash or shouting at her, would only increase her anxiety. The most effective approach is to fatigue her, without giving in to her frenzied behavior in any way. After what seems like an interminable time, she stops struggling and comes up for air.

Janet so far has not interfered, but now she can't hold back anymore. "You're hurting her! She must be in pain if she is screaming this loudly."

My patience is being sorely tested by owner and dog, but I will myself to reply well-nigh calmly, "She is not in pain, believe me. I cannot work with you unless you at least give me the benefit of the doubt. I'll gladly explain the process to you later. But if my approach upsets you, maybe now would be a good time to reconsider training with me."

Over the years I have found that indulging dithering and irrational dog owners, aside from being intensely nauseating, is every bit as ineffective as coddling an already spoiled dog. The owner is a critical factor in the equation of the dog's behavior modification.

"Well, all right," Janet says reluctantly. "Go ahead then."

During our brief verbal interchange, Tigger has had the opportunity to rally some strength.

"Come on," I say, sweet-talking her as I start walking a second time. No way! Tigger enters round number two. She screams like a banshee and bucks like a savage bronco. I remain passive, as before. After five more renditions of this delightful behavior, Tigger stops once again, her flanks heaving and her tongue, by now distinctly blue from lack of oxygen, hanging down to her knees. When the color of her tongue returns to pink, I speak to her gently but firmly and simply start walking. This time she follows me like a lamb. She is in need of a friend now and with a happy wag of her tail accepts my coaxing and patting her.

After arriving at a certain measure of success, it is always opportune to give the dog a well-deserved break. I make use of the time by offering the promised explanation to Janet.

"Tigger is on a regular buckle collar, not even a choke-chain. What could possibly have caused her pain?" I address Janet who doesn't really know what to say.

"Well—er—but why was she screaming?" Jane shakes her head. Now impelled to look beyond her ill-reasoned, superficial pain hypothesis, she hits a little closer to the target. "A temper tantrum?" she provides the answer to her own question.

"In a way, yes. Tigger is startled, anxious and disinclined

to comply. Doubtless, she has had success by voicing her protest before." I pause for effect. Janet does not disappoint me.

"Well, yes," she admits hesitantly.

"Actually," I continue my elucidation, "a display of pain or weakness makes an animal vulnerable. Therefore, dogs are programmed to *hide pain*. Cats are even more proficient at it than dogs. When adult dogs are in serious pain, they are usually silent and withdrawn, sometimes restless. When they scream it is usually in protest or when they are startled. Not infrequently, dogs emit a short scream when they are *overwhelmed* by the sudden onset of sharp pain. Puppies, on the other hand, commonly scream their heads off when they are even in a little bit of discomfort, because this behavior triggers the maternal protective behavior."

"You made your point," Janet admits graciously.

"We go on training? I need to know you are serious about this."

"Absolutely," says Janet and this time she means it.

As soon as Janet takes the leash, as expected, Tigger's legs become dysfunctional once again. This time, however, Janet does not give in. She simply rides out Tigger's resistance, which is by now much shorter and less intense. Within a few minutes Janet, too, is able to walk Tigger all over my training field.

We give Tigger a break, while I discuss her behavior with Janet.

"Your main reason for coming is the fact that Tigger is destructive at home when you leave her, correct?"

"Yes. I would only need to crate her for a few hours every day, but that became such a battle that I gave up. Now I find something she's chewed up every time I come home."

"And what do you do when you find the mess? Do you scold her?"

Dysfunction du jour

"No, not anymore. It's no use anyway. But I'm not pleased, I tell you."

"And Tigger knows it, no doubt!" I say.

Before Janet can deny the veracity of this statement, I go on, "When Tigger was little, did you sometimes scold her when she peed in the house or chewed on something and you found the mess later?"

"Well, sure!" Janet says righteously. "She became housebroken, but she never really stopped chewing on things when no one was looking."

"Janet, Tigger is insecure in your presence and feels the constant need to appease you. This is not only her personality, but also learned behavior. I think that Tigger is anxious about your *coming back*. Your presence is something she views with mixed feelings." I can see that Janet considers the possibility of my having a screw loose, but for now she is willing to give me the benefit of the doubt.

"She has to learn to feel differently about you, and that is not going to be easy. Feelings are not easily changed, yours or hers. You will learn to be her leader by teaching her certain skills and giving her *self-confidence*, and she will begin to see you in a different light."

Janet's homework consists of walking Tigger on-leash and feeding her in an open carrier kennel. Tigger is allowed to keep her rear legs outside in the beginning. If she doesn't eat with at least her head and shoulders in the crate she is not to be fed anywhere else. For now, Janet must not shut Tigger into the crate.

During the next session, Tigger walks obediently, if somewhat submissively, on the leash. When Janet throws a cookie into a crate, Tigger enters and eats her treat. Her back legs, however, stay outside the crate.

"No matter how far back I put the food, she stretches so

255

that she doesn't have to go in completely," Janet reports.

"Well, it's time for another lesson," I say, taking Tigger's leash. Interestingly enough, when I have Tigger on a leash, she vacillates between flatly refusing and relative confidence. The obsequious behavior she displays when she is near Janet is not in evidence. In fact, the farther she is away from Janet, the less fawning she becomes.

When I urge Tigger to go in the crate, of course, she refuses. I simply propel her inside, none too gently, and close the door. Tigger is furious and screams her disapproval.

I'll have none of that! With both fists I execute a drum roll on the roof of the crate, bellowing, "If you don't shut up, the sky is going to fall!"

Tigger is so shocked, she doesn't make another peep.

"Why didn't you throw a treat in the crate to entice her to go in at least halfway?" Janet asks.

"Good question, Janet," I reply. "Normally that would be the appropriate way to *teach* her to go in a crate. Most dogs actually like to be inside a crate, or at least don't mind it. In Tigger's case, however, you have already used treats. She doesn't *want* to go in. Why, I don't know at this time, and it doesn't really matter. Under no circumstances do I want to *trick* her. Dogs aren't stupid. They recognize a trap, and they will distrust the trainer."

"I have done that, you know," Janet admits. "I've thrown a treat in the crate and then shut her in. Now she refuses to go in all the way even if there's food inside."

"Yes, I thought you had probably done that," I nod sagaciously. "Well, time to let the little monster out."

Tigger exits happily and is rewarded for her patience with praise and a bit of running. On my next attempt, Tigger once again refuses, but her resistance is weakening. At my urging, she goes into the crate and is rewarded with a treat.

Dysfunction du jour

A simple "Quiet!" now suffices to prevent her from caterwauling. The subsequent times, Tigger goes into her crate without cringing and without so much as a moment's hesitation.

"In almost three years I have not been able to do what
you have just accomplished in five minutes! You must be
psychic about dogs! Do you hypnotize them?" Janet mar-
vels, half-seriously.

"Absolutely!" I nod. "Madame Vera, canine psychic
extraordinaire, supernatural guidance, clairvoyant readings
of leftover puppy chow, and laying on of hands with the
world-famous patented Magical Touch! Seances daily. All
major credit cards accepted. You didn't know that?"

"Now you're making fun of me." Janet gives me a lop-
sided smile.

"Yes, a little. You don't seriously believe all that—er—
baloney about dog psychics and cures of behavior problems
through massage? Do you?"

What can poor Janet say after my little tirade?

"No, of course not! Well, they should at least call you
the 'dog whisperer'."

Similar nonsense I have heard probably dozens of times
over the years. Fortunately, I don't have what it takes to be
a charlatan.

"I don't think 'whisperer' would be quite appropriate,"
I say with a grin.

Janet unexpectedly has to take a trip. With considerable
trepidation she leaves Tigger at the kennel for a few days.

"You really think she'll be okay?" she frets. "You know
she gets so frantic when she's being left."

"Trust me, Janet, she'll be just fine," I assure her. "I just
want to make sure, I am not treating *you* for separation anxiety, right?"

257

Barking Up the Right Tree

"I know, I know, I'm a neurotic dog owner," she twitters.

If she expects me to wave my hands and deny this, I do not oblige her.

"You don't think she'll forget her training, do you?" Janet is concerned.

"What training? No, Janet I don't think she'll forget how to walk. Besides, the brain isn't like a muscle that atrophies. She'll remember what she has learned."

I don't have much to do with the day-to-day operation of the kennel. That is Betty's domain. Had there been any difficulties with Tigger, however, I would have heard about it immediately. In any event, I do not expect any trouble. Most dogs who allegedly suffer from separation anxiety function quite well in our kennel. Two days after Tigger's arrival I am walking through the kennel. As usual, I say hello to all the regulars and introduce myself to the new ones.

"Who is that new dog in number twenty-four?" I ask Betty on my way out. "She seems rather a nice dog."

Betty stares at me as if I had lost my marbles. "You mean Tigger?" she says frowning.

"Tigger? No, not Tigger. She looks a little like her, but it's not Tigger. This one doesn't act like her at all. It couldn't be—"

"Yes, that's Tigger," Betty insists. "We don't have any other dogs that look remotely like her."

"*That's* Tigger? I didn't even recognize her," I say inanely. "I'm going to have another look." Obstinate to the end.

It's Tigger, indeed. But Tigger the Pathetic now presents herself as Tigger the Exuberant. Just like a few minutes earlier, she greets me joyfully and fearlessly and when I release her, she capers and jumps around with her canine playmates. I expected some slight improvement in her attitude, but her transformation is plainly astounding.

Upon my return to the office and after recovering a bit from my stupefaction, I question Betty further.

"Tigger is this friendly with you and all the other employees?" I am still slightly doubtful.

"Oh yes, she particularly adores Larry, and bugs him for food," Betty nods. "She isn't shy or obsequious at all."

"She hasn't destroyed anything, gnawed at the door or something?"

"No, not at all. We crate her at night, at your request."

"And she goes into her crate without a fuss?"

"Surely," Betty says, probably wondering why I am jumping up and down. "I think she actually likes it in her crate."

"This is difficult to believe. She acts happy and—*normal!*"

"She certainly seems normal," Betty shrugs.

"Not around her owner!"

Admittedly with a certain amount of glee, I report about Tigger's behavior to Janet when she comes to pick her up.

"It's all my fault," Janet says without self-pity. "Well, I'm glad in a way. I am capable of being trained."

"Surely you are!" I concede with more optimism than conviction.

But Janet is as good as her word. Over the next few weeks, she learns to be her dog's leader, as well as to understand and tolerate typical dog behavior. No more hysterics when Tigger chews up a pen or a box of Kleenexes. When Tigger comes to our kennel now, Janet always reports that Tigger is reasonably well-behaved when she is left and a happier dog overall.

The term "separation anxiety" has become a broad term for a variety of disorders. The only thing these syndromes have in common is that the owner's leaving triggers the aberrant behavior. The underlying *cause* usually must be sought somewhere else completely. It is almost *never* because the dog loves too much, as the popular belief would have it. Often quite to the contrary.

In countless cases in my practice, dogs suffering from so-called separation anxiety are *much* more confident and carefree when they are not in the presence of their owners or at home. This is hardly a sign of a dog who misses his owner.

As in Tigger's case, there is often a strong indication that the dog is apprehensive of the owner's *return*. The anxiousness is initiated as soon as the owner leaves.

In these cases two things inevitably come together: a sensitive dog and an overwrought owner. The same dog might do very well with a more understanding owner and the same person might have no problems with a dog of a more emotionally robust nature.

Separation anxiety problems of this nature often cannot be mended by modifying the dog's behavior alone. If the *owner* fails to change his or her behavior profoundly, and above all permanently, success is elusive. Frequently, the slightest slip-up on the owner's part sets in motion the dog's cycle of anxious behavior.

And what about the anti-anxiety drugs so often prescribed these days for separation anxiety? In my experience, they simply sedate the dog into a zombie-like condition. I cannot believe that a dog in such a befuddled state of mind is capable of learning anything. And after all, it is very frequently the *owner* who needs to change his or her behavior. The *dog* is usually acting in a completely understandable and predictable way according to the information he has been given. The crude, albeit very pointed, saying "Garbage in, garbage out" also holds true when raising a dog. By making

Dysfunction du jour

the dog the sole identified patient, we are looking in the wrong direction.

Life With
the Schnauzer Family
Travels With Apache, cont.

After a few pleasant days in Berlin, Apache and I travel southeast to Saxony in my rental car. Wisely, I had invested in a folding crate, which I can stow in the trunk of a small car.

With great anticipation I had plotted a scenic route that would frequently take little back roads through villages and romantic small towns, but I am forced to abandon the project. The cobblestone roads, not repaired since the Roman legions marched on them, often become entirely impassable in the middle of nowhere. Although there are modern construction sites everywhere, the views of what must once have been lovely scenery are dominated by old, rundown factories and aggregates of huge gray concrete apartment blocks resembling prisons. In historic towns like Erfurt and Weimar, the venerable patrician houses are dingy brown with soot and exhaust fumes and in a state of near decay. It will take decades to ameliorate the after-effects of a regime that purported to serve the people.

Apache doesn't care. She is elated to be the only dog and have attention heaped onto her. She can sit in the back seat like a princess being chauffeured, without having to compete for space or attention. So far she has made no attempt to defend the car. Anyone can approach and pet her through the open window. Despite her Schutzhund training requiring a stylized protection sequence, defense is merely a game to her. Although I am not particularly worried about my rental car being stolen, I don't want Apache to be in it should that happen. Fortunately, most places allow dogs. However, at a dog competition the nonparticipating dogs have to be kept away from the exhibition area.

Not too long ago, people might have kept dogs to protect their homes and property; these days most people need a big lock on their kennel so that no one steals the dog. I should have taken Ilka.

Such is my gloomy abstraction as I find myself completely lost in some particularly unalluring outskirts of an East German city at night. I think I do not need to mention that the streetlights are exceedingly sparse and dim.

While I am poring over a map that appears to have no resemblance to reality, a disheveled looking man, probably intoxicated, materializes out of thin air, pokes his head into my half-open window and shouts something unintelligible. Startled and uneasy, I don't really want to open the door. But what if this fellow needs help?

Apache, who had been snoozing on the back seat, unconcerned about my topographical impasse, now without warning shoots forward with a roar. Reflexively, my arm flies up to protect the man's face. But I needn't have bothered. He could not have jerked back more rapidly if I had dropped a hand grenade.

Apache's aggression has matured and erupted just at the right time. Of course, I praise her, and from then on all my worries of her being stolen from my car dissolve.

It is not uncommon that aggression bursts forth suddenly and unexpectedly in a young dog. (The puzzled owner inevitably responds with dog training's most infamous statement: "My dog's never done that before!") Like the proverbial genie released from its bottle, it can never be put back again. Fortunately, with most dogs it can be controlled.

The World Championships for Riesenschnauzer was a successful event. Of the more than fifty dogs entered, Storm and Iro placed somewhere in the middle, not as well as we had hoped, but considering that they had to compete against some of the best and best-trained dogs in the world, it was a satisfactory experience.

My obligation as interpreter and cheerleader safely behind me, I am finally free to spend the rest of my vacation visiting friends from my school and scouting days. I am a little apprehensive in my knowledge that one of them has two children who are "a little afraid of dogs," the other a house with lots of expensive antiques and white couches and carpets and the third one a cat that is unfamiliar with dogs and therefore frightened of them. My proposal to stay in a hotel was categorically denied in all cases.

🐕 🐕 🐕

It is safe to say that my friend's children, although delightful in every other way, are bloody terrified of Apache. On the first day, they press themselves against the opposite wall as soon as we enter the room. If they inadvertently come too close to her, they jump back with a squeal.

The value of having socialized my dogs exclusively with friendly and outgoing children now becomes very apparent. Apache simply ignores my friend's children, having obviously decided that they are not worth the effort. She doesn't react to their bizarre behavior, because it doesn't threaten her. Once the children see that Apache will not pursue them, they become a little less anxious. Of course, I make sure that Apache's boisterous nature finds an outlet by taking her for long walks in the country.

"I'm not sure we'll ever get a dog," my friend informs me, "but if we do, we want one just like Apache!"

You can't *buy* a dog like Apache, I want to say. You choose very carefully a puppy from confident mentally sound parents and shape its behavior with sensitivity to the dog's needs. Instead, I politely (and proudly) reply, "Yes, she is rather a nice dog, isn't she?"

Mixed Emotions

I don't believe in merely patching up symptoms. In my opinion, successful treatment of aberrant behavior must be holistic and structural in its approach. When a system is out of balance, the trainer has to pay attention to all aspects of the dog's personality and disorders in order to improve functionality. Furthermore, in all training, but particularly in treating profoundly behaviorally disturbed dogs, the social structure surrounding the dog—the human pack—also needs to be adjusted if there is to be any lasting improvement in the animal's behavior.

Ryker is not a likable dog. He is a two-year-old, terribly obese, castrated Rottweiler-German Shepherd mix. Just getting acquainted with him sets my teeth on edge. Displaying a rather distorted version of playfulness laced with aggression, he plows into me, and before I can touch him he bolts away. On the next turn he saunters past me, nipping at my hand and quickly sheers off. When I attempt to coax him to me, he backs up, barking wildly and fearfully. Approaching him is impossible. When his owners, a young couple, try to come near him, he plays keep-away, running circles around them with his hackles up and his tail wagging, barking all the while.

Finally, Ruth and her husband Greg are able to trick their dog into letting them catch him. On the leash he vacillates between obstreperous and timid. As soon as I approach, he cowers behind Ruth, and the thought of snapping at me is not very far from his mind.

"He doesn't like other dogs," Ruth tells me. "I can't really walk him anymore at all."

"That's not his only problem. He's a rather screwed-up dog!" Without fail, ever the soul of tact.

"He's pretty naughty, all right," Ruth admits, with a nervous giggle. "I can't really handle him at all, even in the house. Until a few months ago he minded Greg pretty well, but not anymore."

"Yeah," Greg corroborates, "he's really out of control. I travel a lot, but now I'm almost afraid to leave Ruth with him, he's such a handful."

A handful is rather a naive understatement when applied to Ryker. There are so many things wrong with him, I hardly know where to start. This dog is a study of conflicting emotions: social behavior mixed in with aggression, play behavior mixed in with avoidance behavior, fluctuating to unsure aggression. Submissive and dominant behaviors are shifting back and forth. I can't imagine how anyone could live with this nasty creature, who at the moment gives no evidence of any redeeming traits.

As if she were reading my mind, Ruth launches into one excuse after the other. "He is only a little unruly on-leash. Otherwise, he's really sweet when he wants to be, and we love him. He used to be such a darling puppy and—"

"But he isn't anymore. There are major aberrations in his behavior. Ruth, you can't help him become a well-adjusted dog if you close your eyes to his problems."

"I guess we hoped you would tell us it wasn't so bad," Greg comes to his wife's assistance, looking a little disheartened. "We almost got rid of him, but then our vet recommended that we call you."

I am very familiar with this pattern in owner behavior. First, I get a highly emotional phone call in which a distraught owner enumerates a list of imagined and real canine transgressions, claiming he or she has to see me right away because the dog is out of control and the situation has become intolerable. Upon closer inquiry, it is usually revealed that the condition has existed for months and sometimes years! When the owner actually appears for a session with his canine delinquent, he tries to explain away every aberrant behavior.

Recognizing the problems is the first step in finding the key to their solution. But right now, I'm not yet certain where the key is. This dog is crazy. At this time I don't know how much of it was created and how much is due to his inherited, nervous, unstable disposition. Clearly, *all* behavior has a genetic component to it. But some behavior is so strongly influenced by heredity that it cannot be successfully changed.

In Ryker's case there are only two things I know for certain: First, these types of problems get worse over time ... and I hope it is not already too late to effect a significant change.

Second, with confused dogs it is of the utmost importance that the trainer keep a cool head. It is very easy to get drawn into the dog's anxiety and *react* by struggling with all kinds of symptoms at once, without ever getting to the root of the problem. (One might, for instance, begin by punishing or blocking the inappropriate aggression. The result would undoubtedly be more confusion.) The Gordian knot of conflicting emotions has to be somehow unraveled and prevented from tangling over and over again.

"We want you to keep him and train him," Greg informs me.

Unlike Puck, whose only problem behavior was inappropriate aggression toward dogs, Ryker's aggression is merely the tip of the iceberg. When a dog is this confused and shows antisocial behavior to this degree, the suspicion lies near that the owner is part of the predicament. The owner, therefore, must become part of the solution by maintaining a change in his or her behavior.

"You'd be wasting your money," I tell them bluntly. "Ryker's behavior is so much tied to yours that you must be the ones to train him. With my help, of course."

"Do you think we could do that?" Ruth is doubtful, but Greg thinks this a good idea. As so often with couples, the two appear to polarize each other. Where Ruth is nervously giggly and voluble, Greg is calm and taciturn. It is finally decided that Ruth is to carry out the major part of training.

The first objective consists in beginning to lower Ryker's anxiety. There are two main components to this.

One, we have to give him a simple task that consistently provides him with feelings of security and success, as well as pleasure. In his confused state of mind, it is unlikely that he would process even moderately complex signals appropriately.

Two, his exercise regimen has to be increased to such a degree that it effects changes in the brain. There are sound physiological reasons to postulate that prolonged and repeated exercise lowers anxiety. This is one aspect of dog training and behavior modification that is often overlooked, to the dog's detriment. Nearly a hundred years before science proved them right, dog trainers of old maintained, "Movement frees the dog."

We begin with the first phase of the Rocket Recall. Greg holds Ryker and Ruth runs away in a straight line with her pockets full of food. Here already, we confront the first set of problems. Ryker runs for a few yards, but because of his obesity he waddles the rest of the way. When he finally arrives, Ruth flails her hands in his face and attempts to hug him. The dog, naturally, retreats.

Mixed Emotions

Ruth and Greg now get my standard lecture on not reaching for the dog.

"You understand, don't you? Feed close to your body, so he has to make body contact to eat. Prolong his contact with you by feeding him many little treats, one after the other. And finally, under no circumstances reach for Ryker at all!" I counsel for the hundredth time.

Ruth giggles, "Yeah, it's just so hard to remember!"

Greg nods gravely.

"Look Ruth, I know you are nervous, but you have to pull yourself together and concentrate on what you are doing."

When I reveal my diet plan for Ryker—namely, he is not to be fed unless he comes—Ruth demonstrates the usual hand-wringing. Greg thinks the proposal is reasonable.

"As far as the exercise is concerned, you need to trot him on a bicycle," I break the news to them.

"A bicycle?" Ruth exclaims, her eyes as big as saucers. "I can't even walk him on a leash!"

"This is different. You need a device called a 'Springer,' which clamps onto the bicycle frame. The dog is put in a harness and regardless of how much or in which direction he pulls, the bike stays straight, practically effortlessly. The dog cannot get into the wheels or into the pedals or pull you over. It really works."

"If you say so. Okay, we'll do it."

"Ultimately, a dog of his size should be able to run ten to fifteen miles in about two hours a couple of times a week and shorter distances the rest of the time. But Ryker is a long way from that goal. Run him only until he is tired and take a short break, then run him again for a few minutes, slowly building up duration and speed. The first few weeks you may not get much farther than a block or two."

Barking Up the Right Tree

"We probably shouldn't run him when it's hot," Greg observes keenly.

"Of course not. Exercise in the morning or in the evening. Do not let him gallop. Always keep him at a trot; it is the most efficient gait. Keep him on the right side of the bicycle, away from traffic."

"And this will help make him more manageable?" Ruth is not convinced.

"You won't see the benefit for some time. He is so obese and out of shape that it's going to be a slow process. But expending energy, together with giving him (and you) progressively more difficult tasks, *will* make a huge difference. I would like to get him to the point that you can take him for walks off-leash. That way you don't have to run him on the bike as often; it's more fun."

"Walking him off-leash?" Now even Greg shows some animation. "You really think that would be possible? Without him going after other dogs?"

"I think it's possible; we'll have to see. In any event, you have your work cut out for you!"

Although there is some improvement both in Ryker's weight loss and exercise regimen, as well as in his coming more readily and without conflicting emotions to his owners, progress is exceedingly slow. Week after week, I send Greg and Ruth home with the advice to continue in the same vein.

Eventually, as Ryker's weight drops and his responsiveness to food motivation increases, we continue with Sit, Down and Controlled Walking (on the Flexi-line), in addition to the recall.

After several months Ryker's weight is in normal range. He runs next to the bicycle every day for half an hour or more and his understanding of the motivational exercises is very good.

"He is so much easier to deal with," Ruth chatters happily while Greg nods earnestly. "He responds to his name practically all the time, and he is just overall not as crazed as before, and he seems happier. Is it time yet to have him learn to walk off-leash? He is still rather a jerk when he meets another dog."

To substantially progress with Ryker, we have to enter the next phase of training, and I am not looking forward to it.

"Ruth and Greg, you are at a crossroads here." I have a heart-to-heart talk with them. "You could continue with positive motivation for much longer and Ryker's reliability would possibly come up a notch. A small notch. Or you could start to compel obedience with him and make it completely reliable."

"That's what we want. Complete reliability," Greg says without hesitation.

"Not so fast," I reply. "Continued positive motivation wouldn't be as effective as switching to compulsion, but it is by far the easier way to go." Never one to mince words, I go on, "Ryker has a nasty streak a mile wide. He will not take lightly to pressure from you. If you decide to compel obedience, you have to see it through. Half-hearted pressure or failing to persevere until you succeed is going to be worse than nothing."

"I don't quite understand what you mean," Greg says.

"Let's say you command him to lie down. He refuses and you jerk the leash. Now Ryker is ticked off and growls at you or maybe even wants to bite you. If you back off now, he will never forget that he can bully you. You have to come on strongly enough that he knows you mean business,

273

but not so strongly that he panics."

"He's growled at us before," Ruth interjects.

"I'm not surprised to hear it," I nod. "You have made a lot of progress so far. The question is, do you want to solve the rest of the problems, or do you want to learn to circumvent them? It's your decision."

"I don't know," Ruth says, giggling.

"You can do it," Greg tells her.

"Ruth, I don't want you to do it unless you can convince yourself that you are prepared to pull it off. Why don't you two go home and think it over."

"I've decided I want to do it," says Ruth with as much firmness as she can muster.

Oh dear!

Taking a deep breath I manage to utter, "Well—okay. You're *sure* you want to do this?"

"Oh yes!" Ruth nods.

"All right," I say, resigned. "I'll start him. That'll make it easier for you."

First, I encourage Ryker to lie down with food motivation, which he does eagerly and quickly. On my next command, he drops to the ground, but when he sees that no food is forthcoming, he starts to get up. Now I jerk the leash and thunder at him to lie down. Although I am quite strong, Ryker gives no sign that he was in any way impressed by my attempt. My next jerk is designed to make his teeth rattle, but again he ignores it completely. At this rate, my arms will get as long as those of a Neanderthal and Ryker will become even more inured to pressure.

I now equip insensitive Ryker with a pinch collar and try to enforce the Down once more. He ignores my command, but now he is mad. He digs in his heels and glares at

274

me, getting ready for a showdown. At my next snap of the leash he flies forward, teeth bared.

Of course, I have anticipated this and when he lunges, he meets squarely with my boot. *Now* he is impressed. At my next command, he lies down reluctantly. Certainly no praise is warranted at this time, just because the dog forgoes his intent to bite the trainer. After I release him, I repeat the exercise. This time he lies down a bit faster. Although it was less than a perfect performance, now I praise him reassuringly.

It stands to reason that there is a loss of happy working attitude if the dog has to be pressured this profoundly. For now, there is a trade-off between reliability and cheerful attitude, which we will address at a later time.

"Your turn, Ruth," I say handing her the leash.

Ruth commands Ryker to lie down and, naturally, he ignores her.

"Jerk the leash *now!*" I shout at her.

Ruth twitches the leash and giggles.

This is never going to work. I can make one last attempt to pull the rabbit out of the hat. In certain cases and as a last resort when reasoning has proven futile, it is highly successful to provoke dithering owners into redirecting their politely suppressed anger at *me* toward their *dogs* instead. This enables owners to break through the barrier that prevents them from taking charge with their dogs when the circumstances require it. When the owners are not really serious about changing their ineffective and misguided behavior, however, the technique fails. Once there is sulking, or worse there are tears, I concede defeat and send owner and dog on their way.

"If you can't do it, then quit! Stop giggling! If you giggle one more time I'm calling this whole thing off! This is not a kindergarten!" I shout. Just like with dogs, *what* I say is much less important than *how* I say it.

Ruth yells, "Down!" and gives the leash a terrific yank.

Ryker is thoroughly shocked to sense such unexpected rise in his owner's fortitude that he lies down immediately. Ruth herself can hardly believe what just happened. She looks as dumbfounded as her dog.

It is not time yet to let up on the pressure. "Again!" I command sharply.

After two successful repetitions, Ruth releases Ryker to play and I praise her for her newfound mettle.

"When you practice at home, you *must* persist until you get success. Then give Ryker a break. Continue with your recalls with food. If you run into any problems, call me."

The following week Ruth reports that Ryker lay down well when she commanded him over the course of several days. The day before her lesson, however, he once again refused and when she insisted, he growled and snapped at her.

"That is not surprising. Let's hope it's pre-extinctive behavior," I tell them.

"It's what?" both ask in unison.

"His last hurrah. His final attempt at being a nasty little bugger."

"He's growled at Greg and me before, but he has never tried to bite," Ruth sniffs, her eyes brimming with tears. "He is such a timid dog that I didn't really want to push him; I thought he would become even more afraid," Ruth tells me.

"Ruth, you are making an error with serious consequences in your thinking," I explain. "A dog can be skittish and nervous without being submissive. These are two completely different attitudes or frames of mind."

"And he is not submitting to me, right?" Ruth asks.

"Exactly. In all probability, he growls at you not because he is afraid, but because he does not want to submit."

"You don't think we are too hard on him?" Ruth frets.

"Good grief, Ruth! You have never really defied him before. As long as he gets his way he has no reason to threaten you. He is trying, we hope one last time, to re-establish the status quo ante. That is, *you* obeying *him*. Do you really want to be at the mercy of your dog?"

"No we do not!" Greg says decisively.

"I guess not," says Ruth. "I want him to respect me," she amends after a pause, drying her tears.

I don't give up lightly, as long as there is hope for the dog and as long as I sense that the owner is serious about changing the dog's behavior. Between my pressure, cajoling and firmly explaining the process in detail over and over, Ruth continues Ryker's training successfully. We condition him to the remote collar for the recall and work him around other dogs. Being off-leash and with respect for his leaders firmly in his brain, he makes no strong attempt to attack another dog.

As the final phase we increase again the food rewards and are thereby able to instill once more a happy working attitude in addition to reliable obedience.

Although Ryker is doing well in my training areas, we still have to put to the test his behavior and his owners' ability to control him in the real world. We meet in the parking lot of the open space. Ryker is sticking his head out of the car window with a blissful expression, his ears fluttering in the breeze. He looks like a normal happy dog when he greets me with a friendly wagging of his tail. There is no vestige of his old aggression or quirkiness with me.

Now we shall see if his training holds together in the

face of uncontrollable variables. Because of Ryker's unusually high threshold for physical discomfort, we have set the remote collar slightly above a medium level. Ryker knows what to do and his owners have been painstakingly instructed how, and above all *when*, to administer a correction.

Ryker is understandably excited when he smells and sees the woods in front of him.

"At the first sign of inattention—" I admonish, shaking my index finger.

"We know!" Greg interrupts with a grin. "Correct him before he screws up."

Ruth nods, broadcasting her anxiety. "Greg is going to remind me when I get too nervous to react in time."

At the sight of the first dog, Ruth commands Ryker to lie down and he complies willingly. As so often, the other owner makes no attempt to call his dog back, and therefore Ryker is released to meet him. When the two dogs make contact, Ruth stands still, rooted to the ground, staring.

I give her a little shove. "Go! Keep moving!" But like a walking doll whose batteries have run out, Ruth only takes a single step and once again comes to a standstill, gaping at the two dogs. I have to take her by the hand and tow her away. Peering over my shoulder, I can observe Ryker, who is tense but not hostile. When the two dogs are about to disengage, I tell Ruth to call Ryker.

"Ruth, you do remember that once the two dogs meet, you have to keep moving along, don't you? It minimizes the possibility of a fight because your dog does not have the feeling you are supporting him."

"I know, I know," Ruth giggles, but stops when she looks at my face. "I just got nervous and forgot," she says ruefully.

"You also remember that you *must not* correct your dog for disobedience when another dog is greeting him. You must correct him a split second before he bolts up to another dog. Once the two dogs meet, simply walk away, but peek over your shoulder."

"I'll have Greg remind me," Ruth says.

After a short time walking, we encounter a woman with her two West-Highland Terriers. Ruth commands Ryker to lie down. The woman makes no effort to influence her dogs.

Greg is standing in front of Ryker. "Please call your dogs!" he asks the woman. Evidently, he does not yet trust Ryker with two small dogs and he is playing it safe.

The woman calls, and of course, both dogs ignore her and keep scampering toward Ryker. Embarrassed and a bit peeved, the woman runs to seize the little hobgoblins. She grasps one by the collar while she sweeps up the second one. The first one slips out of his collar and while she is attempting to recapture him, the second one bounces out of her arms. She succeeds in hoisting number one and now she scurries after number two, while number one is once more struggling to get away. The scene resembles something out of a mad slapstick movie. Eventually, she contrives to restrain both and drag them away.

Finally, Ruth has a chance to use the collar. A little farther down the path a lady with three medium-sized dogs comes into view. The dogs are running circles and wrestling with each other. This is too much for Ryker. He bolts toward the dogs who are at least twenty-five yards away. His action was easy to anticipate and Ruth calls Ryker immediately. He ignores her and keeps on going. Now Ruth corrects him by pressing the button and calls him again. Ryker returns forthwith. All of this happens much faster than I can describe it. We are still more than twenty yards distant from the dog trio down the trail.

"You did it, Ruth," I am elated to tell her, "with absolutely perfect timing!"

Ruth herself can hardly believe it. "Yes, I did, didn't I?" she chatters happily.

"Ruth, don't bliss out now. Watch your dog!" Enough already of this soft-soaping.

Much to my surprise the lady with the three dogs has them completely under control. She calls them to her and walks toward us with her obedient dogs by her side.

"My dogs are friendly," she tells us as she approaches.

"Actually, so is this one," I answer quickly in Ruth's place. "We just don't want him to bolt up to other dogs."

"No," the lady replies, "I don't like mine to do that either."

We release the dogs and after an initial moment of uncertainty, Ryker begins to play with the trio.

Ah, the rare joys of civilized interaction with another dog owner!

The next few encounters are, I am happy to report, unremarkable. Greg is helping Ruth a bit with her timing. But as the tension in Ruth subsides, she handles most of the situations appropriately without help.

She calls Ryker to her when we see another dog. If the dog approaches, Ryker is released. Although Ryker is allowed to meet most dogs, it is always Ruth's decision to give him permission.

On the way back we meet the woman with the two little white terriers once more. Ruth orders Ryker to lie down.

"You again!" The woman blurts out in exasperation as she is making another red-faced attempt to dash after her dogs.

I am reasonably sure that Ryker will leave the terrible terrier twins unscathed and give Ruth a sign to release him. We move ahead and Ruth calls Ryker, who streaks toward us, the Westies in his wake. The little munchkins are not done playing yet and have no desire to return to their owner. They'd probably have followed us, or rather Ryker, to the parking lot. Greg catches one and I hold the other, and we deliver the little devils to their flustered owner.

Back in the parking lot I tell them, "Congratulations, you've just graduated, or rather, you have earned the right to practice on your own."

A couple of months later Greg calls me to report that Ruth has been able to take Ryker for walks off-leash every day without his support. She had to correct him with the collar during the first week only two or three times.

"That's the way it is supposed to work, Greg. If you had to correct him on every walk, we would have to do some remedial work."

"You know, Ryker is now a joy to be around. He is easy-going in the house and we don't really worry about other dogs anymore on our walks. He responds to Ruth and me immediately," he reports. "Do you remember what he was like before?" Greg asks, and I can almost see him shaking his head.

How could I forget! "I remember."

"It's hard to believe he's the same dog. We really *like* him now!"

Life With
the Schnauzer Family
Travels With Apache, conclusion

Southward-bound to Freiburg and the Black Forest at last. The vaunted German autobahn has indeed no overall speed limit, but that hardly matters. One can barely drive for a couple of miles without getting stuck in endless traffic jams.

Although I had prophylactically made hotel reservations, it turns out that Apache ignores my friends' cat completely—somewhat to my surprise, because at home the Schnauzer Family used to take rather devious pleasure in tormenting my cat Havoc. In order to spare my poor feline a life of being permanently marooned on the refrigerator, I had found her a new home. Here, however, Apache acknowledges the territorial claim of the resident cat and the two casually stay out of each other's way. Whereas with my other friends, Apache was mostly just tolerated, here she is allowed on the couch and beds and fed ample treats; of course, she takes shameless advantage of my friends' love for animals.

"Oh dear," my friend observes, "Apache is hungry." Apache, indeed, is sitting on the couch, drooling and keenly ogling the loaded breakfast table with greedy eyes. Without delay, my friend butters a roll and puts an extra slice of ham on it. "Here, little Indian, you don't have to live like a dog," she coos as Apache grabs the roll from her hand and swallows it whole with gluttonous abandon. She doesn't want to forfeit precious time by chewing; another delicacy might be imminent. Ilka didn't raise any stupid puppies and Apache knows a softy when she sees one. She continues to drool and reaps another roll with a choice cold-cut.

Well, there is a quaint German proverb that says that eating and drinking keep body and soul together, and clearly, every effort is made to prove its veracity. I console myself that a day of hiking in the Black Forest Mountains will probably use up the excess calories, both for Apache and me.

Frequently, my training students report proudly that their dogs are never fed at the table and get only dog food to eat. Dogs, however, can be perfectly trained not to beg when they are told. My dogs understand very well that certain things, like lying on the bed or getting a tidbit off the table, are privileges, not rights. They accept me as their leader and I exercise the leader's prerogative to make these decisions.

The dictum that one must never feed anything but dog food, which has been cooked at high temperatures, dehydrated, pressed into pellets that look like deer droppings, and preserved to have a longer half-life than plutonium, is of course a ploy the multibillion-dollar dog-food industry foists on the consumer. Often, with such a continual one-sided (and often fat-laden) diet, dogs lose or never develop the ability to digest a variety of food. The slightest change in diet results in intestinal upsets, such as vomiting, diarrhea, or worse.

Dogs have evolved from predators to semi-solitary scavengers. Should wild or feral dogs be lucky enough to kill or steal a prey animal, they first eat the stomach contents of the killed herbivore. They also eat diverse roots, fruit and berries, as well as pilfer anything remotely edible from garbage dumps. It stands to reason that a diet consisting of diverse wholesome fresh foods is infinitely better for the dog than a preserved, dried mixture of generally unrecognizable low-grade ingredients. A low-fat fresh diet that consists of one-third protein and two-thirds cooked whole grains and greens serves dogs very well. I sometimes fall back on an easy compromise: I use small amounts of a high quality, low-fat, low-protein kibble and add meat, fish or cottage cheese, brown rice or other cereals or noodles and cooked or raw vegetables. So-called table scraps are never thrown away (as long as they are not fatty or highly spiced), but mixed into the dog meal. Bones are strictly forbidden, except very large beef-shank bones trimmed of fat. The rule is this: Gnawing bones is good, because it cleans the dog's teeth; eating bones is potentially dangerous, because it can cause very serious intestinal injuries.

We spend the day scaling the windswept heights of the Feldberg and hiking down to the glacier lake called, rather romantically, "the dark eye of the mountain." On three sides surrounded by sheer granite walls, it is almost round, its nearly black surface betraying its immense depth, and it is ice cold. Even my little water-rat Apache is satisfied with a short swim.

In the evening my friends and I treat ourselves to a nice dinner. The restaurant is not four-star, but definitely of the white-tablecloth, starched-napkin variety. While we peruse the menu, Apache at her usual station, quietly under the table, the landlord appears. "Your dog is so well-behaved," he begins.

(Good thing he didn't see her begging and drooling on the couch this morning.)

"Would she like a bone?" he asks.

"A bone? What kind of a bone? Well—yes, I guess—but

no pork chop or rib bones. They splinter and are dangerous for dogs."

"I'll show you." The landlord disappears and shortly after emerges with a monstrous bone. It must be the whole leg of a cow.

"Not here," the man says reasonably, when Apache sniffs the bone excitedly. "Out in the hall."

"The entrance hall?" I inquire. "Not a good idea. If someone approached her or tried to pet her while she was gnawing on *this* bone, she might take offense."

"Yes, right. The balcony then. You can sit so that you can see her through the window."

In America I am so very accustomed to keeping a low profile when taking my dog into public areas, for fear we might be told to leave. And now, looking at the landlord holding a huge bone in the middle of the dining room, I cannot shake the feeling that I am playing the straight part in a British comedy. Surely any time now, the senior singles ladies' historical society will charge in on stilts and attack us with their handbags in a reenactment of the battle of Hastings.

But the other diners either smile or ignore us. Apache gets her bone on the balcony and we our garlic-laden snail ragout in hot ceramic bowls accompanied by a dry Riesling.

Westward, along terraced hills cultivated with Riesling and Sylvaner grapes and across the Rhine to France. Through the town of Munster, on to the Vosges Mountains where we are planning to hike for a few days. One does not need a map to find the town. When the wind is off the cheese factory, one simply follows the scent. Now, the French Munster cheese has no resemblance to its nearly tasteless, odorless American cousin, called muenster. The real Munster variety is *serious* cheese!

Travels With Apache, conclusion

Apache has no eyes for the exceptional beauty of the countryside; as long as there are mice and squirrels to hunt, she is happy. The Vosges Mountains are vaster and far less tourist-infested than the Black Forest. The occasional hiker we meet greets us with a friendly *bonjour*, but that is the only indication we have changed countries.

So far I have not had to communicate much in French, much to my satisfaction. After studying the language for five years in school, a long time ago, I have at my disposal a rather esoteric vocabulary and no ability to understand French if it is not spoken with a thick German accent. Therefore, I rely heavily on reading body language, tone of voice and facial expressions, much like a dog does with humans.

After a day of hiking we need to be fortified with some coffee and cake. For this purpose we enter a cafe in a small village. My friend, who speaks French fluently, uses the washroom after my reassurance that I am up to the task of ordering coffee. How hard can it be?

"Deux cafes, s'il vous plait," I say artfully to the waitress in my most careful pronunciation, doing my level best to appear urbane.

But the waitress is not listening. She peers at Apache, who is rather tiredly reposing under the table. Smiling beatifically, the young woman asks in a mild voice, *"Votre chien, est-ce-qu'il mechant?"*

Relying on her amiable tone of voice, I smile back and respond, "Oui, oui." (It sounds more like wee-wee, I'm afraid.)

The young waitress slams her order book on the table and leaps back, now shrieking, at the top of her lungs, *"IL EST MECHANT?"*

Good grief! What? What did I say? People are beginning to stare. Sluggishly, somewhere in the recesses of my mind, a nebulous memory surfaces. *Mechant? Mechant?* Oh, shit!

Barking Up the Right Tree

Vicious, it means vicious!

Waving my hands maniacally I shout, *"Non, non, non! Pas mechant! Pas mechant!"* Now all eyes are on us.

The waitress approaches cautiously, *"Il est gentil?"*

Dare I agree? Having what seems like thousands of pairs of eyes staring at me is not exactly conducive to my presence of mind. It will be my fault if French-German detente is failing and the progress of the European Union is thwarted.

"Oui, oui, tres gentil. Pardonnez-moi, je ... j'ai ... je n'ai pas compris," I stammer, my cosmopolitan affectation having all but gone to the dogs. *"Regardez!"* I add, patting Apache on the head by way of substantiating my assertion.

Evidently the young woman believes me, because now a remarkable change comes over her. She squats in front of Apache, stroking her and jabbering something about *"petit toutou."*

Little toutou bears all this with her usual complaisance.

Epilogue

Of the old guard—the Schnauzer Family, the German Shepherd Dogs Grendel, Ben, Gandhi, and Falko, and the Dobermann Schnupp—only Apache is still alive. She is now almost thirteen and in superb shape, vivacious and athletic. Only her grizzled prickly beard and eyebrows betray that she is no longer in her prime. She still steals knives and spatulas out of the sink, but has given up on hiding them.

My beloved Ammo died of a heart attack at the age of eight.

Ilka died at the age of fourteen and a half. She had a tumor in her abdomen and I had her euthanized to spare her prolonged suffering.

Not a day goes by when I don't miss them all.

As much as I would have enjoyed raising another litter keeping Ilka's and Apache's bloodline alive, I have decided that selling puppies is not for me. I love raising them, but I am much too anxious about placing them in just the right home, and even then I can't help feeling as if I'm selling my charges into bondage. Yet, keeping them all is not a reasonable option. If only I could order just one or two puppies for myself! Fortunately, not all responsible, knowledgeable breeders are as neurotic as I am or we would soon run out of good working dogs.

After Ilka's death I bought a new Riesenschnauzer puppy in Germany. Hexer is a young dog right after my heart; he is enthusiastic, easily motivated and very trusting. Whereas my Ammo was mostly inadvertently funny, Hexer is an inveterate clown and enjoys nothing more than playing to the crowd. He is always in a cheerful mood and he makes me laugh. I adore him. Apache, in her new role as Grand Dame, is doing her best to teach her ward the importance of respect and how to steal utensils out of the sink. I have no doubt that with her and my concerted efforts, Hexer will turn out to be a splendid dog. But that is going to be another story.